Quick Start Guide to JavaFX™

About the Author

J.F. DiMarzio is a seasoned developer. He began developing in BASIC on the TRS-80 Color Computer II in 1984. Since then, DiMarzio has worked in the technology departments of companies such as the U.S. Department of Defense and the Walt Disney Company. He continues to strive to push the limits of technology and develop on new, emerging platforms.

DiMarzio is also an accomplished author. Over the last 12 years, he has released 11 books, including the first edition of *JavaFX: A Beginner's Guide*. His books have been translated into four different languages and published worldwide. DiMarzio's writing style is very easy to read and understand, which makes the information in the topics he presents more retainable.

About the Technical Editor

Simon Ritter is the manager of the Java Technology Evangelist team at Oracle Corporation. Simon has been in the IT business since 1984 and holds a Bachelor of Science degree in Physics from Brunel University in the U.K.

Originally working in the area of UNIX development for AT&T UNIX System Labs and then Novell, Simon moved to Sun in 1996. At this time he started working with Java technology and has spent time working both in Java development and consultancy. Having moved to Oracle as part of the Sun acquisition, he now focuses on the core Java platform, Java for client applications, and embedded Java. He also continues to develop demonstrations that push the boundaries of Java for applications, such as gestural interfaces, embedded robot controllers, and in-car systems. Follow Simon on Twitter, @speakjava, and visit his blog at blogs.oracle.com/speakjava.

ORACLE®   *Oracle Press*™

Quick Start Guide to JavaFX™

J. F. DiMarzio

Mc
Graw
Hill
Education

New York   Chicago   San Francisco
Athens   London   Madrid   Mexico City
Milan   New Delhi   Singapore   Sydney   Toronto

Library of Congress Cataloging-in-Publication Data

DiMarzio, J. F.
  Quick start guide to JavaFX / J.F. DiMarzio.
      pages cm
  Includes index.
  ISBN 978-0-07-180896-5 (paperback)
  1. Java (Computer program language)   2. JavaFX (Electronic resource)   3. Graphical user interfaces (Computer systems)   I. Title.
  QA76.73.J38D559 2014
  005.13'3—dc23

                                                                          2014001068

McGraw-Hill Education books are available at special quantity discounts to use as premiums and sales promotions, or for use in corporate training programs. To contact a representative, please visit the Contact Us pages at www.mhprofessional.com.

Quick Start Guide to JavaFX™

1234567890   DOC DOC   10987654

ISBN   978-0-07-180896-5
MHID   0-07-180896-5

Sponsoring Editor Brandi Shailer	**Technical Editor** Simon Ritter	**Production Supervisor** Jean Bodeaux
Editorial Supervisor Patty Mon	**Copy Editor** Bart Reed	**Composition** Cenveo Publisher Services
Project Manager Harleen Chopra, Cenveo® Publisher Services	**Proofreader** Susie Elkind	**Illustration** Cenveo Publisher Services
Acquisitions Coordinator Amanda Russell	**Indexer** Ted Laux	**Art Director, Cover** Jeff Weeks

Neil, a great ally and agent over the last ten years.

Contents at a Glance

Contents

Introduction

Why This Book?

Welcome to *Quick Start Guide to JavaFX*. This book has been designed to give you the best first step into the exciting new frontier of JavaFX 8 development. JavaFX is a rich environment tool, and learning JavaFX is a must for anyone who wants to create immersive, interactive environments for users of any background.

If you are familiar with previous versions of JavaFX, this book is a must have. The platform has undergone major changes with the release of Java 8. *Quick Start Guide to JavaFX* covers the changes to JavaFX and prepares you for real-world development situations on this incredible platform.

This book takes you through JavaFX 8 in a logical manner. It begins by explaining the technology behind JavaFX. You will quickly move into installing the JavaFX development environment and tools. Although multiple development environments are available for JavaFX, the focus of this book is on teaching you the basics of NetBeans. NetBeans offers a rich, full-featured product that is easy to learn and will get you up and running in JavaFX in no time. By the end of the book, you are lead expertly into more complex examples to test your growing knowledge of developing rich JavaFX applications.

Some chapters also include a "Try This" section to help you practice what you have learned. The "Try This" sections are structured like a textbook in that you will be presented with tasks to complete on your own. In addition, each chapter has a "Self Test" section that provides quiz-style questions to further enhance your learning experience. Taking full advantage of the chapter questions and "Try This" exercises will give you a chance to refine your newly acquired skills and create your own applications.

Although this book is not an advanced programmer's reference, you should possess certain skills to get the most from *Quick Start Guide to JavaFX*. Foremost of these, given that JavaFX is now packaged with Java, is Java programming fundamentals. Knowledge of Java classes and basic types will help you understand some of the concepts in this book more easily.

Any comments, questions, or suggestions about any of the material in this book can be sent directly to the author at jfdimarzio@jfdimarzio.com.

Chapter 1
Introduction to JavaFX

Key Skills & Concepts

- Installing JavaFX

- Installing NetBeans

- Using NetBeans

Welcome to *Quick Start Guide to JavaFX*. I am sure you are anxious to begin your journey into the exciting world of JavaFX development, and this is the perfect place to start. Before you begin, you need to have a fully capable development environment. This chapter covers the basic knowledge needed to create and establish a JavaFX development environment that allows you to create excitingly rich interactive applications. It also answers many of the questions you may have about what JavaFX does, and how it does it.

What Is JavaFX?

If you have ever played an Adobe Flash game or have seen an application in Microsoft Silverlight, you have a pretty good idea of products that are similar to JavaFX. I know, it's not fair to compare JavaFX to these other environments, but if you have never seen JavaFX before, I have to compare it to *something*. Now that JavaFX is in its third exciting iteration, chances are you have run into it somewhere.

JavaFX delivers full-featured, interactive experiences to users in much the same way as Flash or Silverlight. However, one of the major differences between JavaFX and the others is that JavaFX is platform independent. Because JavaFX is now fully integrated with the Java Runtime, any device or system that can run Java can also serve up JavaFX experiences.

NOTE

Many changes have been made to the JavaFX platform between versions 1, 2, and now 3. If you have some experience with an older version of JavaFX, or possibly even with the first edition of this book, you should pay close attention because much of what you may have used before is very different now. Also, the third version of JavaFX is now officially known as JavaFX 8, because it is now part of Java 8.

What Is Needed for JavaFX Development?

Before you jump right into development, you should examine the list of requirements as outlined in this section. Think of them as the prerequisites for a successful and rewarding learning process. You should have at least a basic knowledge of the following skills as well as access to the listed software.

Required Skills and Knowledge

Prior development experience is not required to follow along with this book. Even if you've created a single application or developed a basic web page, you still have the skills needed to learn JavaFX. The examples and lessons in this book are specifically designed to teach you JavaFX development.

That being said, any experience you have in Java development is going to help you grasp the concepts of JavaFX even faster. A basic knowledge of the following concepts, although not necessary, will help you get up to speed even faster:

- **Java development**   JavaFX and Java share more than just their root names. If you have ever written a Java applet—and, more importantly, deployed a Java applet to a web page—you should easily understand the deployment process for JavaFX. Previous versions of JavaFX used a proprietary language called JavaFX Script. This has been changed for a more unified, cross-platform Java experience. The JavaFX Script language was replaced with the Java API to facilitate a more unified and simplified programming experience.

- **Cascading Style Sheets (CSS)**   The look and feel of a JavaFX app can be modified using Cascading Style Sheets, or CSS. Development platforms such as HTML can implement CSS as a way to embellish the look of a user interface. JavaFX is no exception, and any experience you have with CSS will definitely be a plus.

- **NetBeans**   Although JavaFX can be developed in almost any integrated development environment (IDE), or even in a simple text editor, the preferred method of development in this book is NetBeans. If you've never used NetBeans before, fear not—this book will walk you through everything you need to know.

These skills are by no means required, and a lack in any of these areas will not affect your ability to learn JavaFX. Whether you are a seasoned professional developer or a novice who has yet to write your first application, you will be able to easily develop in JavaFX after reading this book. The next section lists the software you will be working with in this book to develop JavaFX.

Required Software

This section serves as a brief introduction to the software you will be using throughout this book. A few different software elements are used in JavaFX development, and you will be very familiar with them by the end of this chapter. Don't worry if you do not have any of these software elements yet or have never even heard of one or two of them. By the end of this chapter you will have downloaded and installed all the software required to facilitate JavaFX development.

● **JavaFX SDK** The JavaFX SDK (Software Development Kit) is the major package needed for JavaFX development. The JavaFX SDK contains all the items needed to develop JavaFX applications using JavaFX Script.

● **Java SE JDK** The Java SE JDK (Standard Edition Java Development Kit) is required to compile your JavaFX Script into executable code. The JDK is the base for all Java development.

● **NetBeans** NetBeans is the development environment you will use to create your JavaFX apps. Think of NetBeans as a specialized text editor that can use both the JavaFX SDK and the Java SE JDK to compile text into an executable app.

All the pieces of software listed here are free and can be easily downloaded. The next section of this chapter walks you through downloading and installing the required software.

Required Hardware

This section quickly outlines some of the hardware requirements for running JavaFX. Keep in mind that JavaFX (and Java in general) run on a wide array of hardware and hardware configurations. However, there are some hardware suggestions for getting the most out of your JavaFX.

In general, JavaFX will run on any hardware that is running a supported operating system. To enjoy the performance of the new hardware acceleration pipeline, you will need to follow these recommendations.

Graphics Card	GPU
NVIDIA	**Mobile GPUs:** GeForce 8M and 100M series or higher, NVS 2100M series or higher, and Mobility Quadro FX 300M series or higher **Desktop GPUs:** GeForce 8 and 100 series or higher **Workstation GPUs:** Quadro FX 300 series or higher
ATI	**Mobile GPUs:** Mobility Radeon HD 3000, 4000, and 5000 series **Desktop GPUs:** Radeon HD 2400, 3000, 4000, 5000, and 6000 series
Intel	**Mobile GPUs:** GMA 4500MHD and GMA HD **Desktop GPUs:** GMA 4500 and GMA HD

Downloading and Installing the Required Software

The easiest way to begin is to download and install the latest version of NetBeans. At the time this book was written, the latest version was NetBeans 7.1.2. This version can be downloaded bundled with the latest versions of Java, and thus, JavaFX. This provides for an easy way to get all of the required software installed in one action.

NetBeans

NetBeans is an open-source IDE that can be used for developing on many different platforms. NetBeans can be used for C/C++, Java, JavaScript, and PHP development, as well as JavaFX. When following the examples in this book, you will do all your JavaFX development within a NetBeans workspace.

The first step is to download the latest version of NetBeans for JavaFX. The latest version of NetBeans can be downloaded from www.netbeans.org or from a bundle link provided from the JavaFX download page.

CAUTION

The latest version of NetBeans, at the time this book was written, was the NetBeans 7.1.2 Beta for JavaFX. NetBeans can be downloaded for different languages, and for the purposes of this book, you need to download the version of NetBeans 7.1.2 that is specifically for JavaFX. This will make more sense when you visit the NetBeans download page.

Once you are at the NetBeans download page, the choice of available packages may seem daunting. Fear not, because there is only one flavor of NetBeans 7.1.2 you need to worry about. You want to download the NetBeans IDE for JavaFX (see Figure 1-1).

CAUTION

The download from NetBeans labeled "All" is the version of NetBeans for all available technologies. All the examples in this book will still work if you happen to download this version, but you should try to stick with the NetBeans IDE for JavaFX.

Simply follow the installation wizard and you should have no problem successfully preparing NetBeans for development. The installation wizard will recommend default locations for the installation of the NetBeans IDE and the Java JDK; just accept the default locations, and the remainder of the installation will be a breeze.

Figure 1-1   NetBeans download page

NOTE

If Java has never been installed on your computer, you may need to manually install the latest JDK before installing NetBeans.

When the NetBeans installation is complete, the NetBeans IDE should auto-start. If NetBeans does not restart, you may need to bring it up manually. The NetBeans IDE will open to the development start page (see Figure 1-2). The purpose of the NetBeans start page is to offer you tips and news about developing in NetBeans and JavaFX.

At this point, NetBeans is configured and ready for use. The NetBeans installer will ask you to register NetBeans. This step is suggested but not required. Registering your product will give you access to news about upgrades and the NetBeans forums.

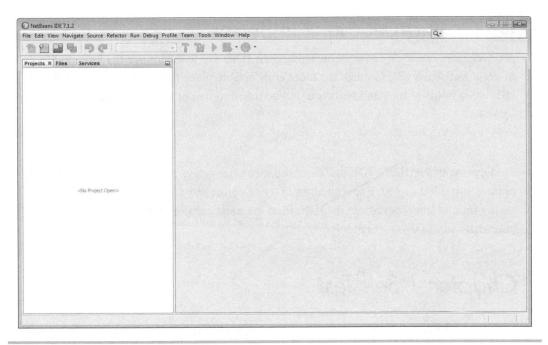

Figure 1-2   The NetBeans default start page

Ask the Expert

Q: **Do I have to use NetBeans for JavaFX development?**

A: No, JavaFX can be developed outside of NetBeans. All you really need to write in JavaFX is a simple text editor, the Java JDK, and the JavaFX SDK. However, developing outside of NetBeans would require a fairly good knowledge of command-line compiling in Java.

Q: **Can any other IDEs be used for JavaFX development?**

A: Yes, you can also use Eclipse. Eclipse is another open-source IDE that would require the use of a plug-in to work with JavaFX. However, at the time this book was written, no plug-in was available for JavaFX 2 (and above) and Eclipse.

Try This Configure Your NetBeans

A developer should be comfortable using their IDE. Try to customize the look and feel of your NetBeans IDE to make it a more comfortable place for you to work. When your IDE has a familiar look and feel, you will be much more apt to have creative development sessions.

Open your NetBeans IDE and from the menu bar select Tools | Options. Explore the options provided to you. Experiment with these options by setting different ones and taking note of how they affect the IDE. Find the most comfortable options for you and your method of development.

Chapter 1 Self Test

1. What is the name of the open-source development environment you will use throughout this book?
2. True or false? You should download the version of NetBeans for All Developers.
3. True or false? The Java JDK will be installed for you automatically if needed (if you have the JRE installed).
4. Which NetBeans settings can you accept the default values for during installation?
5. What is the difference between the JavaFX SDK and the Java JDK?
6. What is the purpose of the NetBeans start page?
7. True or false? You must successfully register NetBeans before using it.
8. At what website is NetBeans available?
9. Name two other applications that closely resemble the functionality of JavaFX.
10. True or false? JavaFX is developed in JavaFX Script.

Chapter 2
Setting the Scene

Key Skills & Concepts

- Creating a JavaFX project in NetBeans
- What is a Stage?
- What is a Scene?
- Running a JavaFX application

In this chapter you learn how to set up a new JavaFX project in NetBeans. JavaFX projects can be confusing for beginners, and sorting through some of that confusion will help you follow the rest of this book. This chapter walks you through, step by step, the process of creating your first project, discovering what a Stage and a Scene are, and running the application.

Creating a New JavaFX Project

If you have not already, open your copy of NetBeans. You will create a new JavaFX project for this chapter using NetBeans.

NOTE
You will use the project created in this section throughout this book. As you progress through the book, you will continue to add application files for the examples in each chapter.

With your NetBeans IDE open, click File | New Project (or press CTRL-SHIFT-N), as shown in Figure 2-1.

Selecting New Project will open the New Project Wizard. Notice that the New Project Wizard contains multiple project categories. This is because NetBeans is used for more than just JavaFX development. You need to select the Categories option of JavaFX and the Projects option of JavaFX FXML Application, as shown in Figure 2-2. Ensure these are selected and click Next. If these options are not selected, choose them now.

The next step in the wizard is the Name and Location step. NetBeans is looking for a name for your project. Name your project **JavaFXForBeginners**. This is a good, descriptive name for your project that will make it easy to identify.

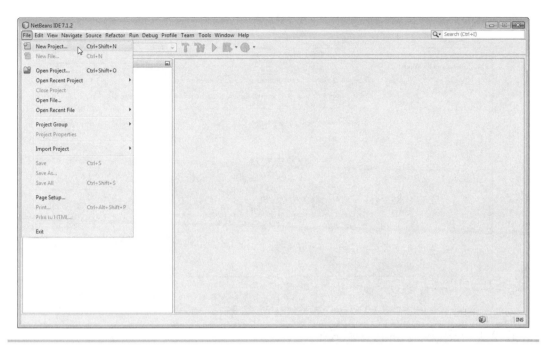

Figure 2-1   Creating a new project

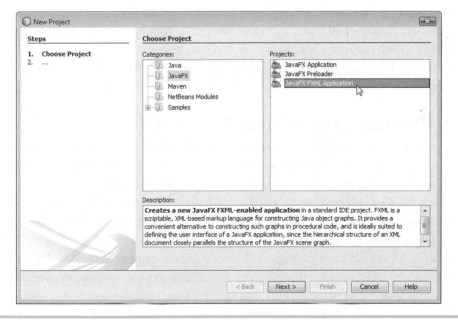

Figure 2-2   The New Project selection window

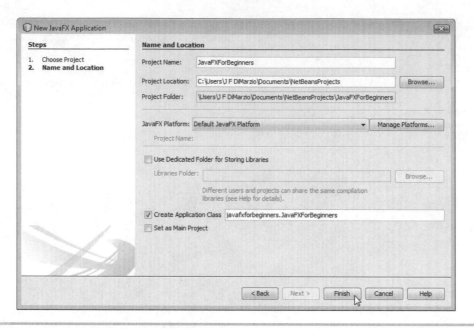

Figure 2-3 The Name and Location step

You should accept all of the remaining default values in this wizard. NetBeans will automatically select the default version of JavaFX and the options needed to create your main project settings.

Feel free to accept all of the defaults in this step. Your Name and Location step should appear as shown in Figure 2-3.

Click the Finish button to create your empty project. In the following section, you will add a package and files to your project.

The (Not-so) Empty JavaFX Project

Once your new project is created, the New Project Wizard will return you to the NetBeans IDE, as shown in Figure 2-4. On the left side of the screen is the Projects explorer frame. Your JavaFXForBeginners project will be displayed in this frame.

Click the plus sign next to the JavaFXForBeginners folder. This will expose the Source Packages folder. The Source Packages folder will contain the packages for your project.

A Java package is a full collection of classes (or in this case, JavaFX source files) that are all related. All the files in a package will be compiled together into a JAR (Java Archive) file and can be referenced in other projects. If you have worked with another platform such as Silverlight or .NET, you can think of a Java package as equivalent to a namespace.

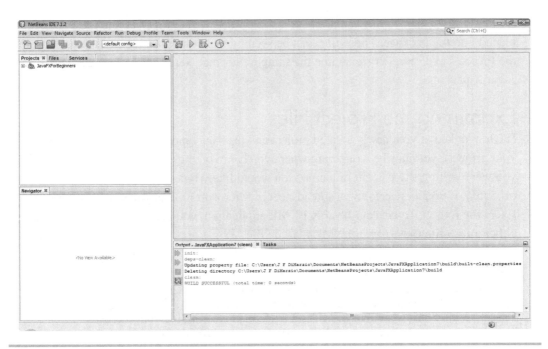

Figure 2-4   The NetBeans IDE with a new project

For example, if you were building a set of Java classes that calculate the area of a shape, you could build them into a specific "area calculator" package. This namespace, and all the classes in it, could then be compiled into a JAR file. You could then use that JAR file in any project where you want to be able to calculate area simply by including the JAR file and referencing the namespace.

Packages have a naming convention you will need to adhere to in JavaFX. A package is named using a hierarchical domain structure that represents you as a developer. Much like a website URL in reverse, the namespace name should begin with the top-level domain followed by the related domain names. For this project we will use the following package:

```
javafxforbeginners
```

TIP

By convention, all Java namespace and project names should be lowercase. For more information about Java naming conventions, visit http://java.sun.com/docs/codeconv/html/CodeConventions.doc8.html.

If you examine the Source Packages folder of the JavaFXForBeginners project, you will see that you have a package for your source files called javafxforbeginners. NetBeans created this package during the project creation process, and three sample files were placed into the package. These files can be seen by expanding the view of the package in the Projects explorer. Let's examine the sample files that NetBeans has placed into your JavaFX package.

Examining the Project Files

Having looked at your newly created project and package (and the three files that are in your project), you may be wondering where you begin typing your code. For example, if you were writing a document or memo, you would likely type into a text document file (.txt or .docx). If you were creating a spreadsheet in Microsoft Office, you would type into an Excel file (.xlsx). To create a JavaFX FXML application, you need to add your code into either a Java file (.java) or an FXML markup file (.fxml).

NOTE

In earlier versions of JavaFX, you would have written JavaFX Script into .fx files. JavaFX now has its own Java SDK, and the code is written in Java into .java files. Therefore, throughout this book, when your code files are referred to as Java files and not JavaFX files, this is not a mistake; you are truly programming your JavaFX in Java.

Take a look at the javafxforbeginners package; you will be able to quickly determine that NetBeans has supplied you with two .java files and an .fxml file. Double-click on the JavaForBeginners.java file to open it in the NetBeans editor. The file should appear similar to what's shown in Figure 2-5.

NOTE

Your screen may differ slightly from that in Figure 2-5.

Your new Java file should be open in the main panel of the NetBeans IDE. In the following sections, you will take a quick tour of the code inside this file, the NetBeans IDE, and you will compile your first JavaFX FXML application.

Exploring the Project in NetBeans

You should now have a shell of a JavaFX FXML project open in your NetBeans IDE, with a handful of sample files generated for you. Your NetBeans JavaFX FXML project should look like Figure 2-5. You might think that an empty project would not be that interesting, and for the most part you are right. However, there are some features and areas of the IDE that you should become familiar with before you begin coding.

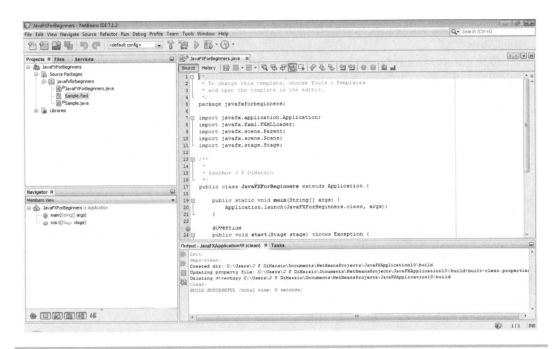

Figure 2-5   The JavaFxForBeginners.java file

For much of your development work in JavaFX, you will be focusing on two areas of the NetBeans IDE. The left side of the NetBeans IDE shows a trio of tabs, labeled Projects, Files, and Services. This set of explorers, shown in Figure 2-6, will be your main mechanism for navigating through your projects.

It is not uncommon for projects to start off very small and end up using many files—from code to images and configurations. The explorers help you keep track of these files.

Figure 2-6   The Projects, Files, and Services explorers

They also allow you to move quickly between files, letting you easily work on different files as needed.

One great feature of these explorers in NetBeans is that they allow you to work with multiple projects at the same time. If you have two projects open in the same IDE, you can easily work with them simultaneously without worrying about closing or opening them. This becomes a very handy tool the more you begin to work in NetBeans.

The second area you will become very familiar with by the end of this book is the Palette section. The Palette, pictured in Figure 2-7, is located on the right side of the NetBeans IDE, opposite the explorers.

NOTE
If the Palette is not visible on your IDE, you can open it by going to Window | Palette or using CTRL-SHIFT-8.

When populated, the Palette contains collapsible tabs of code snippets. You will find yourself using these snippets throughout your code, and extensively throughout the early chapters of this book.

Figure 2-7 The Palette

A snippet, like those found in the Palette, is a prewritten, reusable piece of code. A snippet is very much like one of those "fill-in-the-missing-word" comics. In other words, it is a small section of code with a few pieces of key information left for you to provide. These snippets make it extremely easy for anyone to pick up JavaFX for the first time and produce some very functional applications with minimal effort.

As you progress through this book, you will be introduced to many of the snippets in the Palette. They provide a simple foundation for many of the projects covered in the following chapters. Take some time out to expand each of the Palette categories and explore the snippets included for you.

Working with the JavaFXForBeginners.java File

This section walks you through the code that is in the JavaFXForBeginners.java file that was created in the last section. Believe it or not, even though you didn't write a single line of code, this file has done a lot.

Right now, the top section of your file will look similar to this:

```
/*
 * To change this template, choose Tools | Templates
 * and open the template in the editor.
 */
package javafxforbeginners;

import javafx.application.Application;
import javafx.fxml.FXMLLoader;
import javafx.scene.Parent;
import javafx.scene.Scene;
import javafx.stage.Stage;

/**
 *
 * @author J F DiMarzio
 */
```

The following sections explain the layout and purpose of this section of the file.

The Comments

The first four lines of code in your Java file are the opening comments. Comments are not lines of code. In fact, comments are ignored by the compiler. So why bother using them? Comments are added to a file to explain the purpose of the code within the file. They are solely for the benefit of people reading the script files, not the compiler.

The beginning comments that have been added to your file read as follows:

```
/*
 * To change this template, choose Tools | Templates
 * and open the template in the editor.
 */
```

By Java coding standards, your beginning comments should include the class's name, version, and creation/modification dates, as well as any copyright information you may want to include.

Take a look at the first two and the last two characters of the comments that were added to your file. The first two characters are /* and the last two characters are */. All your multiline comments must begin and end with these characters, respectively. All the other asterisks you see in the comments (at the start of each new line) are added purely for embellishment and readability.

Typically, comments are added to explain the purpose of a script file as a whole, or possibly larger sections of code. For example, place your cursor at the end of the comment line where your name appears and press the ENTER key. Highlight the template comments that were added to your file and replace them with the following:

```
/*
 * JavaFXForBeginners.java
 *
 * v1.0 - J. F. DiMarzio
 *
 * 7/16/2012 - created
 *
 * Sample JavaFX code from Chapter 1 of 'JavaFX
 * A Beginner's Guide'
 */

//BEGIN CODE
```

You have just added some standard Java beginning comments to your script file. These comments describe your file as being version 1.0 of the file named JavaFXForBeginners. java. The creation date and a short description (in place of the copyright notice) close out the comments.

After the description, we have added a single-line comment marking the start of the code. This is not part of the Java standard; rather, it was put here to show you how to create a single-line comment. Notice that single-line comments being with // rather than /*. Also, because they are only on one line, there is no need to close them. As such, anything on that line will be considered a comment.

In the next section, you will learn about the package statement.

The package Statement

After the beginning comments is the following line:

```
package javafxforbeginners;
```

This line, while having very little direct impact on your code, can teach you some key points about programming in Java. The core purpose of this line is to tell the compiler that all the code under this line belongs to the javafxforbeginners package. The package declaration must be at the top of the .java file.

This line of code has three important components you should be aware of. The first word of the line, "package," is a Java keyword. Keywords are special commands that have a predefined meaning to the Java compiler. They are also known as "reserved." As such, they cannot be used elsewhere in your code as variable names or anything other than their predefined purpose. The keyword package tells the compiler that anything following the keyword is the name of the package.

The name of your package follows the package keyword (in this case, javafxforbeginners). Because the purpose of the keyword is to tell the compiler that everything after it is the name of the package, the compiler needs to know where the end of the filename should be. Otherwise, by definition, the compiler would think all the code in the file was the package name. Therefore, Java has a special character set aside as a statement terminator: the semicolon (;). The statement terminator tells the compiler when it has reached the end of a specific line of code. Although there are very specific exceptions to this rule, you will need to end your code statements with a semicolon to let the compiler know you have finished. If you do not use a semicolon where one is expected, the compiler will give you an error when you attempt to compile.

TIP

Compiling is the process where your code is converted from human-readable text to a class file containing bytecodes that can be executed by the Java Virtual Machine.

In the final sections of this chapter, you will examine the functional code that is in the JavaFXForBeginners.java file.

Your First Stage

All JavaFX applications are built on a Stage. The naming of this container, as the Stage, is very apropos. Think of the Stage as the foundation for the rest of your application's objects. Just as with a dramatic production, the action happens on a stage—and JavaFX is no exception. All of your action is going to take place on a Stage.

The Application Entry Point

After the package statement is a set of import statements. These import statements are used to help the compiler resolve references to methods without the need for fully qualified paths. That is, without using import statements, you would have to type out the entire path to an external method. This could make your code rather verbose and possibly unruly.

```
import javafx.application.Application;
import javafx.fxml.FXMLLoader;
import javafx.scene.Parent;
import javafx.scene.Scene;
import javafx.stage.Stage;
```

After the import statements, you will see the code of the file. The code begins with a class declaration for the JavaFXForBeginners class.

```
public class JavaFXForBeginners extends Application {
    public static void main(String[] args) {
        Application.launch(JavaFXForBeginners.class, args);
    }

    @Override
    public void start(Stage stage) throws Exception {
        Parent root = FXMLLoader.load(getClass().getResource("Sample.fxml"));

        stage.setScene(new Scene(root));
        stage.show();
    }
}
```

The JavaFXForBeginners class extends Application. This means that the JavaFXForBeginners class inherits all of the public, protected, and package scoped variables and methods of the Application class. This is important to know because it is required for your main application class to extend Application for it to run correctly.

Within the JavaFXForBeginners class you will see two methods: the main() method and the start() method. The main() method is executed when your application starts up. Within the main() method is one method call to launch(). One interesting fact here is that in the latest version of Java FX, main() is no longer required. It is included only for backwards compatibility. The main() method is the entry point of the application, or the point at which the Java Virtual Machine will begin execution. In this case, the JavaFXForBeginners class is being passed as the start of the JavaFX application. Why not just start the JavaFX application automatically? The functionality being separated out allows you to run other Java methods or to thread other JavaFX applications from the same main() method.

The launch() method will now look at the JavaFXForBeginners class, ensure that it extends Application, and then attempt to call the start() method which JavaFXForBeginners inherits from Application. Your JavaFX application must override the start() method to execute any code you want to run.

In the sample code provided by NetBeans, you can see that within the start() method a file named Sample.fxml is loaded, the Scene is set on the Stage, and the Stage is shown to the world. This is all the code that is needed in your class to start a basic JavaFX application.

Let's now take a look at what is in the Sample.fxml file to see what this file's role is in the application.

The Sample.fxml File

The Sample.fxml file, created by NetBeans during the JavaFX FXML Application process, contains the following code:

```xml
<?xml version="1.0" encoding="UTF-8"?>

<?import java.lang.*?>
<?import javafx.scene.*?>
<?import javafx.scene.control.*?>
<?import javafx.scene.layout.*?>

<AnchorPane id="AnchorPane" prefHeight="200" prefWidth="320"
xmlns:fx="http://javafx.com/fxml" fx:controller="javafxforbeginners.Sample">
<children>
<Button id="button" layoutX="126" layoutY="90" text="Click Me!"
onAction="#handleButtonAction" fx:id="button" />
<Label id="label" layoutX="126" layoutY="120" minHeight="16" minWidth="69"
prefHeight="16" prefWidth="69" fx:id="label" />
</children>
</AnchorPane>
```

FXML is a user interface (UI) markup language based on XML. FXML is a great language for creating easy, quick, and flexible UIs for your JavaFX application. If you have experience with XML or any other markup language, then FXML will look very familiar to you and will be very easy to pick up and understand.

There are two important things to note in this file. The first is the controller assignment:

```
fx:controller="javafxforbeginners.Sample"
```

This line tells JavaFX that a class named Sample is part of the javafxforbeginners package, which contains all of the code for the elements in the FXML. Take a quick look at the Projects explorer and you will see that, indeed, you have a file named Sample.java. This file contains the Sample class.

The second thing to notice about this file is the elements that have been placed on the UI. The Sample.fxml file contains two interactive elements: a button and a label. The button contains a handler that, in turn, calls to the Sample class. Let's take a look now at the code in the Sample class—in the Sample.java file—and see what the handle for this button does.

The Sample.java file contains the code that is referenced by the elements in the Sample.fxml file. If you have done any web development before, or are familiar with other web development languages, you can think of Sample.java as the "code-behind file" for Sample.fxml.

Open Sample.java in NetBeans. The file contains a class named Sample. The Sample class has the following code:

```java
public class Sample implements Initializable {

    @FXML
    private Label label;

    @FXML
    private void handleButtonAction(ActionEvent event) {
        System.out.println("You clicked me!");
        label.setText("Hello World!");
    }

    @Override
    public void initialize(URL url, ResourceBundle rb) {
        // TODO
    }
}
```

Without even knowing JavaFX, you should be able to see that when the button in Sample.fxml is clicked, the application is told to print the words "You clicked me!" and then the text of the label is set to "Hello World!" Because you will learn about how the code works throughout this book, we are not going to dive into that topic here. Rather, let's compile this application and see it in action.

Figure 2-8   Your first compiled JavaFX application

Compiling Your JavaFX Application

To compile your JavaFX application and run it, press the F6 key. You can also click the large green arrow in the NetBeans menu bar. Either of these methods will compile your script into an executable application.

Your code will compile and run based on the selected Run Configuration, and the result will be displayed as a separate window.

NOTE
Currently, you only have one Run Configuration: <default>. As you progress through the book, you will create others.

In this case, your first JavaFX application will create a very exciting window with a single button. Clicking the button will produce the message shown in Figure 2-8.

In the next chapter, you will create your own "Hello World" application.

Chapter 2 Self Test

1. What is the name of the frame where all your projects are listed?

2. What is the name of the wizard used to create a new JavaFX project?

3. What is another name for a namespace?

4. Which panel of the NetBeans IDE lets you navigate through code samples?

5. True or false? The Palette panel contains predefined pieces of reusable code.

6. What file extension is assigned to JavaFX code files?

7. What type of word is "package" in the Java language?

8. What markup language is FXML based on?

9. What are the beginning and ending characters for comments?

10. True or false? You cannot use a code-behind file when using FXML.

Chapter 3
Hello World

Key Skills & Concepts

- Learning what is MVC
- Using JavaFX Scene Builder
- Binding values

In this chapter you will start writing code in your JavaFX application. This is where all the prerequisite work from the previous two chapters begins to pay off. All of the time and effort you put into learning the basics in the first two chapters will help you master the Java, JavaFX, and FXML introduced in this chapter.

The best part of learning a new language is getting to express your thoughts and visions in a new and exciting way. That is exactly what you will be doing in this chapter. You will learn how to start taking things you may (or may not) know how to do in other languages and bring them to life in JavaFX. But first, we need to discuss some key concepts.

What Is MVC?

Since version 2, JavaFX has followed the Model-View-Controller (MVC) design pattern, which was created to separate the UI of an application from the business logic. This allows user interfaces to be designed and built independently of the logic that will be used to control them. MVC is not unique to JavaFX or FXML. This design patter has been around for many years and is used on almost all major frameworks. However, if you are not familiar with it, fear not: You will pick up much of what you need to know as you work through the examples in this book.

When you're using FXML, the .fxml file represents the "view" of MVC. This means that the FXML file is the physical view of the data or logic that is being represented by the UI. You can design and create user interfaces in an FXML file without the need to know the underlying data of the related Java files. You will see this process more in depth in this chapter when you are introduced to a new tool called JavaFX Scene Builder.

The .java file that is tightly coupled with the .fxml file is the "controller" of the MVC pattern. The controller takes data and information from the business logic and passes it to the view. In the default Hello World application that NetBeans created for you, the Sample.java file is the controller to the Sample.fxml view.

Finally, any of the supporting Java files in your project that contain logic or data that is displayed in the view are the "models" in the MVC pattern. The model can be spread across any number of files in your project as long as they are all contained in the same namespace.

In the next section of this chapter you learn how to use the JavaFX Scene Builder to design and create an FXML view as referenced in the MVC pattern.

Using JavaFX Scene Builder

Oracle has made available a tool for graphically designing and developing the UI of your JavaFX application. JavaFX Scene Builder is designed to work directly with your FXML files and allows you to add, remove, and manipulate the elements in your FXML. In this section, you will use the JavaFX Scene Builder to modify the Sample.fxml file and create a new Hello World application.

NOTE

Download the JavaFX Scene Builder at http://www.oracle.com/technetwork/java/javafx/overview/index.html.

After downloading and installing JavaFX Scene Builder, use it to open the Sample.fxml file in your JavaFXForBeginners project. You should see a screen like the one shown in Figure 3-1.

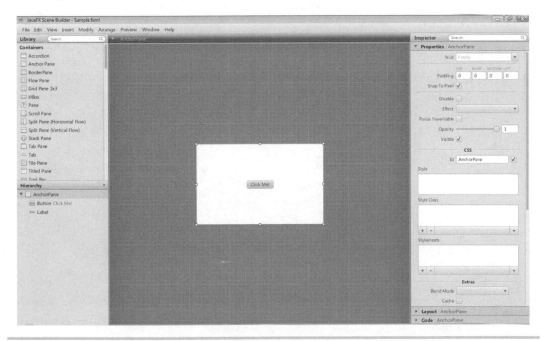

Figure 3-1 Sample.fxml in the designer window

Remember the sample Hello World application that NetBeans created for you in the last chapter? That JavaFX application had a button in the center with the text "Click Me!" You can clearly see this button in the JavaFX Scene Builder.

Working with Containers

On the left side of the JavaFX Scene Builder designer window are two panel views: Library and Hierarchy. Figure 3-2 illustrates these views.

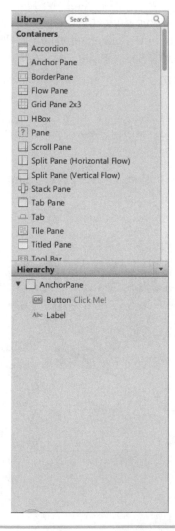

Figure 3-2   The Library and Hierarchy views

The view you want to focus on right now is the Hierarchy panel view, which shows you all of the elements on your FXML file in a nested list form. Looking at the view for the Sample.fxml file, as it is right now, you should see an AnchorPane element. Within the AnchorPane are a Button element and a Label element.

Clicking each of these elements in the Hierarchy view will highlight the corresponding element on the FXML designer. Highlighting any given element will populate the Inspector view on the right side of the JavaFX Scene Builder. The Inspector view is illustrated in Figure 3-3.

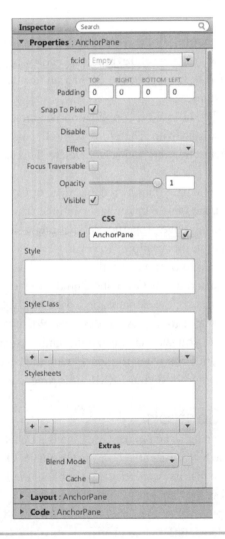

Figure 3-3   The Inspector view

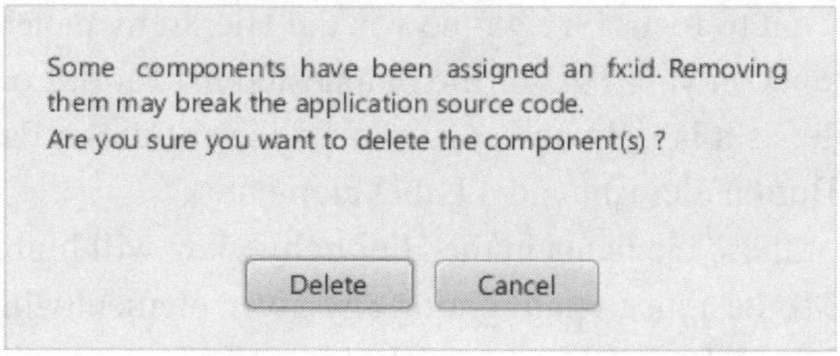

Some components have been assigned an fx:id. Removing them may break the application source code.
Are you sure you want to delete the component(s) ?

Delete   Cancel

Figure 3-4   A warning message

The Inspector view contains all the assignable properties of the highlighted element. Within the Inspector view you can set, review, and modify any property of any element in your FXML file. This makes JavaFX Scene Builder an invaluable tool when designing and creating JavaFX applications.

For the purposes of the Hello World application you are creating in this chapter, you will need a clean canvas to start with. Therefore, right-click both the Button element and the Label element in the Hierarchy view and select Delete. This will remove these elements from Sample.fxml.

While deleting the elements, you may receive an error like the one shown in Figure 3-4. If you get this error, click the Delete button and continue. This error is just telling you that the elements you are deleting have properties set that might tie them to your code. We will address the code later in this section. However, if we did not address the code, your application would not compile or run correctly.

Now you are going to add a new GridPane element to the Sample.fxml. A grid pane provides a good way to organize the elements on a page neatly. Click the GridPane 2×3 item in the Library view and drag it to the FXML designer. When you have it lined up with the center of the AnchorPane, you will see horizontal and vertical snap lines, as shown in Figure 3-5. Drop the GridPane when it lines up with the center of the AnchorPane.

With the GridPane anchored to your FXML, it is time to add some controls.

Working with Controls

The first control you are going to add to the GridPane is a Label. Click a Label control in the Library and drag it to the bottom-right cell of the GridPane. Once the Label is anchored into your grid, select it so that its properties are visible in the Inspector view. You need to set some properties before moving on.

Currently, the Text property of the Label control is set to "Label." This means that when the control is rendered, unless you change the text, the Label will read "Label." Let's change that by deleting the text in the Text property. Next, near the bottom of the Inspector view is a collapsed pane labeled Layout. Click the arrow next to Layout to expand it.

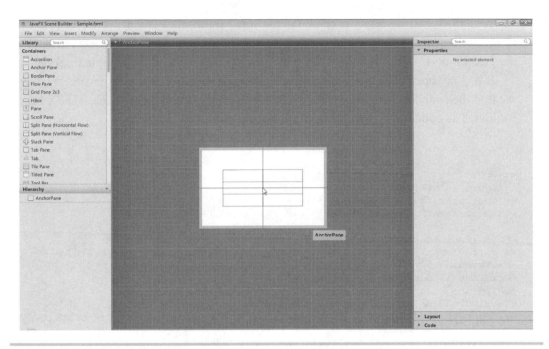

Figure 3-5   Centering the GridPane

Once the Layout pane is expanded, you need to set the GridPane constraints. Ideally, you want the Label to expand to fit the text that displays, yet stay centered within the GridPane cell it has been placed in. To do this, set the Hgrow and Vgrow properties to ALWAYS, and set the Halignment and Valignment properties to CENTER. This is shown in Figure 3-6.

Figure 3-6   The GridPane constraints

With the Label set, add a TextField to the upper-right cell. The only property you want to edit right now for the TextField is Text. Just as you did for the Label, delete the text in the Text property of the TextField. Save the changes you made to the Sample.fxml file.

If it is not open already, open NetBeans to your JaveFXForBeginners project. You will see that the code for Sample.fxml now reflects the changes you made in the JavaFX Scene Builder. The code for the Sample.fxml file should appear as follows:

```xml
<?xml version="1.0" encoding="UTF-8"?>

<?import java.lang.*?>
<?import javafx.scene.*?>
<?import javafx.scene.control.*?>
<?import javafx.scene.layout.*?>

<AnchorPane id="AnchorPane" prefHeight="200.0" prefWidth="320.0"
xmlns:fx="http://javafx.com/fxml" fx:controller="javafxforbeginners.Sample">
<children>
<GridPane layoutX="60.0" layoutY="55.0">
<children>
<Label GridPane.columnIndex="1" GridPane.halignment="CENTER"
GridPane.hgrow="ALWAYS" GridPane.rowIndex="2" GridPane.valignment="CENTER"
GridPane.vgrow="ALWAYS" />
<TextField prefWidth="200.0" GridPane.columnIndex="1"
 GridPane.rowIndex="0" />
</children>
<columnConstraints>
<ColumnConstraints hgrow="SOMETIMES" minWidth="10.0" prefWidth="100.0" />
<ColumnConstraints hgrow="SOMETIMES" minWidth="10.0" prefWidth="100.0" />
</columnConstraints>
<rowConstraints>
<RowConstraints minHeight="10.0" prefHeight="30.0" vgrow="SOMETIMES" />
<RowConstraints minHeight="10.0" prefHeight="30.0" vgrow="SOMETIMES" />
<RowConstraints minHeight="10.0" prefHeight="30.0" vgrow="SOMETIMES" />
</rowConstraints>
</GridPane>
</children>
</AnchorPane>
```

Feel free to compile and run your project now. Even with the existing sample code in the controller, it will still compile correctly and run. When your JavaFX application starts, you should see a TextField that you can enter text into. In the next section you learn how to use binding when turning this TextField into a Hello World application.

Creating Your Own Hello World Application

The most common form of human expression is the use of words. The main method of communicating your ideas to others is through words and sentences. We are bombarded with information via words every day. Whether you are listening to music, driving in your car, surfing the Web, or developing code, you are using and digesting words. Regardless of whether the words are spoken or written, the best way to get a point across is to use words.

For this reason, you will learn how to write text to the screen using JavaFX. Chances are, no matter what type of application or rich environment you want to create in JavaFX, you will need to write some form of text to the screen. Writing text to the screen is a common, everyday task in development. Therefore, let's start writing text using JavaFX.

In the last section, you added a TextField and a Label to the Sample.fxml file. Now you will use binding to link the two controls together.

Using JavaFX Binding

Binding allows you to link properties and values in such a way that a property is dynamically updated when a value changes. Therefore, rather than you having to write code that listens for a change in a property, reacts to that change, writes the value out to another property, and then redraws the application, you only need to bind the property to the value and the rest is taken care of for you.

You are going to bind the text property of the Label on your Sample.fxml file to the Text value of the TextField. By binding these controls, whatever you type in the TextField will dynamically be displayed in the Label. Let's take a look at how this kind of binding is accomplished. The syntax used in binding is as follows:

```
${<control.value>}
```

The $ (dollar sign) operator is used in binding for variable resolution. The $ operator tells JavaFX that anything following it should be considered a variable. To resolve a controller property value, you must wrap the controller name and the property in braces:

```
{...}
```

CAUTION
There are obviously times when you would want to use $ and not mean it to resolve to a variable, such as when you want to write out a dollar amount. In these cases, you need to escape the default functionality by placing the escape character (\) before the dollar sign (\$).

Take a look at your current control code in the Sample.fxml file in NetBeans:

```
<children>
<Label GridPane.columnIndex="1" GridPane.halignment="CENTER"
GridPane.hgrow="ALWAYS" GridPane.rowIndex="2" GridPane.valignment="CENTER"
GridPane.vgrow="ALWAYS" text="" />
<TextField prefWidth="200.0" GridPane.columnIndex="1"
 GridPane.rowIndex="0" />
</children>
```

The first thing you want to do is assign an ID to your TextField. Assigning an ID to your TextField will allow you to reference it in the binding. Without an ID, JavaFX would not understand what control you were trying to bind to. Add the following property to your TextField:

```
fx:id="textfield"
```

We chose a fairly simplistic ID here—just "textfield." Feel free to be as descriptive in your naming as you need to. For example, if you were building a larger application with multiple TextFields, you would definitely require an ID that is more descriptive. However, for this small sample application, we are safe with "textfield."

Your new code should appear as follows:

```
<children>
<Label GridPane.columnIndex="1" GridPane.halignment="CENTER"
GridPane.hgrow="ALWAYS" GridPane.rowIndex="2" GridPane.valignment="CENTER"
GridPane.vgrow="ALWAYS" text="" />
<TextField prefWidth="200.0" GridPane.columnIndex="1" GridPane.rowIndex="0"
fx:id="textfield" />
</children>
```

With the ID of the TextField set, we can bind the text property of the Label to it. Using the syntax discussed earlier, the binding should look like this:

```
${textfield.text}
```

Add this binding to the text property of the Label, as follows:

```
<children>
<Label GridPane.columnIndex="1" GridPane.halignment="CENTER"
GridPane.hgrow="ALWAYS" GridPane.rowIndex="2" GridPane.valignment="CENTER"
GridPane.vgrow="ALWAYS" text="${textfield.text}" />
<TextField prefWidth="200.0" GridPane.columnIndex="1" GridPane.rowIndex="0"
fx:id="textfield" />
</children>
```

That is all the code you need to bind these controls. Compile and run your application. When the application executes, type "Hello World!" in the TextField and you should see the results illustrated in Figure 3-7.

In the next section, you will bind to the value that is in your .java file.

Figure 3-7 A binding Hello World application

An Introduction to Methods and Properties

Before you can bind to a value in the controller, you need to understand two Java concepts: methods and properties. The combination of these two concepts will allow you to bind a value from the controller side to the Label on the view. In this example, when you bind from the controller to the view, you are going to bind to a method on the controller. The method, in turn, will reference a property on the controller that produces the value that is then sent to the view. It may sound complicated, but it is not that bad. The next section contains a quick primer on methods.

Java Methods

A method in Java is a sequence of statements that can be invoked by referencing the method's name. When a method is finished executing, it returns a value back to the code that called it. The value that is returned from a method could be of a specific data type, such as String, or it could be nothing. All methods also have what is called a "signature." The signature makes the method unique within the class where it is declared. The signature consists of the method name, the type and number of parameters passed to the method, and its return type. This complex "signature" allows you to have multiple methods with the same name, but different parameters, in the same class.

The syntax for declaring a method is as follows:

```
<modifier><return type><method name>(<parameters>)
{
     <body>
}
```

The modifier can be public, private, protected, or package scoped (declared without a modifier). The modifier dictates what execution security will be placed on the method. Simply stated, a modifier of public dictates that the method can be executed from outside of the class it is defined in, whereas a modifier of private will restrict execution of the method to code within the same class. You will only be dealing with these two modifiers in this book, to make life a little easier.

The return type is the data type of the value that is returned when the method finishes executing. As stated earlier, this can be any valid data type, such a String, double, or int. However, what would you do if your method does not return a value? In some cases, you may want your method to perform a calculation and return to you the result of that calculation. In other cases, you want to create a method that just manipulates some code and does not really need to return anything. In this scenario, you use the return type void to tell Java that your method does not return a value.

The method name is the name used to call your method from other areas of the code. The method name can be anything you want, but try to keep it within some standard guidelines. By coding standards, the name of a method should be a verb or action word, such as "get," "run," "lock," or even "delete." If your method name contains more than one word, the first word should be lowercased and the first letter of the following words should be uppercased, as in getMyValue.

CAUTION
The return type, method name, and parameters together form the method's signature. This is important to know because you cannot have two methods (visible to each other) with the same signature.

After the name of the method is a pair of parentheses, which either can be empty, meaning that no parameters are needed to run the method, or can encompass a set of parameters. If parameters are defined, the values for these parameters must be provided when the method is called.

Finally, after the parameters is the body of the method. The body is the code that does all of the work in the method.

A simple method declaration would appear as follows:

```
public String getMessage()
{
    String message = "FOO!";
    return message
}
```

In the next section, you learn about properties and then combine a property with a method to create a new binding.

JavaFX Properties

A property is a key/value pair that allows you to store and recall a piece of data. Think of a property as a way of storing values that can then be manipulated and retrieved later. Although this is definitely a more advanced topic, it may help you to know that in Java properties are stored in a hashtable. You can imagine a key being used to store and retrieve a specific value from a table—that is a basic property.

When you define a property, you typically need to also define a getter and a setter. The getter retrieves the value of the property for you, whereas the setter sets and modifies it. The code required to create a property may look a little daunting at first, but if you take a minute to look it over, all of the pieces will make sense.

Next, we'll build a property with a getter and setter, and then build a method to call them.

Building Your Property and Method(s)

Let's build a property that is set with a default value of "Hello World". First, open your Sample.java file that was created in NetBeans. Locate the following lines of code and delete them from the file (they are not necessary for what we are doing):

```
import javafx.event.ActionEvent;
import javafx.fxml.FXML;
import javafx.scene.control.Label;
...
@FXML
private Label label;

@FXML
private void handleButtonAction(ActionEvent event) {
    System.out.println("You clicked me!");
    label.setText("Hello");
}
```

With these items removed, your file should look like this:

```
package javafxforbeginners;

import java.net.URL;
import java.util.ResourceBundle;
import javafx.fxml.Initializable;


public class Sample implements Initializable {

    @Override
    public void initialize(URL url, ResourceBundle rb) {
```

```
        // TODO
    }

}
```

Now, let's create our property. You are going to create a property that contains the string value "Hello World".

First, you need to add some new imports to your file. Import the following lines to give yourself access to the code for creating a StringProperty:

```
import javafx.beans.property.SimpleStringProperty;
import javafx.beans.property.StringProperty;
```

Next, create an instantiation of the StringProperty and assign it the default value of "Hello World". The name of the property will be helloMessage.

```
private StringProperty helloMessage =
        new SimpleStringProperty("Hello World");
```

Now you have to create the getter and the setter for this property. The getter and setter are methods that retrieve or modify the value of the helloMessage property.

```
public String getHelloMessage()
    {
        return helloMessage.get();
    }
public void setHelloMessage(String newString)
    {
        helloMessage.set(newString);
    }
```

The getter is a method named getHelloMessage(). Notice that the method returns a String value. The value it returns is the value that is currently assigned to helloMessage. The setter, on the other hand, does not return anything. Therefore, it has a return type of void. The setter accepts a String parameter and then assigns that parameter to helloMessage as its new value.

NOTE

You will not be using either the getter or the setter in the binding directly; however, the property itself will not work unless they are defined.

That is all you need to create the parameter. Your finished Sample.java file should appear as follows:

```java
package javafxforbeginners;
import java.net.URL;
import java.util.ResourceBundle;
import javafx.beans.property.SimpleStringProperty;
import javafx.beans.property.StringProperty;
import javafx.fxml.Initializable;

public class Sample implements Initializable {
    private StringProperty helloMessage =
            new SimpleStringProperty("Hello World");
    public String getHelloMessage()
    {
        return helloMessage.get();
    }
    public void setHelloMessage(String newString)
    {
        helloMessage.set(newString);
    }
    @Override
    public void initialize(URL url, ResourceBundle rb) {
        // TODO
    }
}
```

It is time to bind to the parameter. Let's see what happens when we bind to the parameter from the Label in the FXML.

Binding to the helloMessage Property

With the code in Sample.java complete, switch back to Sample.fxlm to implement the binding on the Label. The syntax for binding to the helloMessage property is as follows:

```
${controller.helloMessage}
```

This statement says that the retrieve should get the helloMessage property of the controller that is defined in the FXML. In this case, looking at the controller property of the AnchorPane, you can see that the Sample class (located in Sample.java) is defined as the controller for the Sample.fxml view:

```
fx:controller="javafxforbeginners.Sample"
```

Modify your Label so that the text property now points to the new binding:

```
<Label GridPane.columnIndex="1" GridPane.halignment="CENTER"
GridPane.hgrow="ALWAYS" GridPane.rowIndex="2" GridPane.
valignment="CENTER"
GridPane.vgrow="ALWAYS" text="${controller.helloMessage}" />
```

Compile and run your application. You should see the message "Hello World" print to the screen through the Label.

In the next chapter, you will learn about JavaFX layouts.

Chapter 3 Self Test

1. What is the purpose of the MCV pattern?

2. What does MVC stand for?

3. In JavaFX, what part of MVC does the FXML represent?

4. What tool is used to edit FXML files?

5. What is binding in JavaFX?

6. True or false? The syntax for binding is #{value}.

7. What is the $ operator known as in JavaFX?

8. What is a method in Java?

9. What is a property in JavaFX?

10. True or false? To bind to a property on a controller, you have to tell the FXML what file your property is in.

Chapter 4
Using JavaFX Layouts

Key Skills & Concepts

- Arranging nodes in a Scene
- Using the HBox
- Nested layouts

Throughout this book, you have learned how to create and use nodes. At its core, JavaFX would not be very interesting without the ability to place these nodes on the screen. Nodes need to be placed logically on the screen for any user interface (UI) to be intuitive and usable.

To this point in the book, you have manually placed nodes within the context of a Scene. Then, using the x and y coordinates of the desired position, you have moved the nodes around to put them in a logical place. However, manually moving nodes around the screen can be a tedious task and ultimately takes away from the time needed to develop functionality.

JavaFX provides a handful of very useful tools to help you organize the placement of nodes on the screen. Layouts can automatically organize your nodes into predefined patterns that will give your applications a professional look and a higher degree of usability.

In this chapter, you learn how to use layouts to organize the various nodes. The first layout you learn about is the HBox.

Before you begin, create a new, empty JavaFX app named **Chapter4**. The .java file should look like this:

```
package Chapter4;

import javafx.application.Application;
import javafx.stage.Stage;

/**
 *
 * @author J F DiMarzio
 */
public class Chapter4 extends Application {

    /**
     * @param args the command line arguments
     */
```

```java
    public static void main(String[] args) {
        launch(args);
    }

    @Override
    public void start(Stage primaryStage) {
        primaryStage.show();
    }
}
```

The HBox

The HBox is a horizontal layout you can use to place relatively positioned nodes on the screen. That is, the HBox layout organizes your nodes next to each other horizontally. To demonstrate this, let's create a Scene with Text and Button elements, as follows:

```java
Text text = new Text();
Button btn = new Button();
text.setText("Sample Text");
btn.setText("Button");
```

Your full file should now look like this:

```java
package Chapter4;

import javafx.application.Application;
import javafx.scene.Scene;
import javafx.scene.control.Button;
import javafx.scene.layout.StackPane;
import javafx.scene.text.Text;
import javafx.stage.Stage;

/**
 *
 * @author J F DiMarzio
 */
public class Chapter4 extends Application {

    /**
     * @param args the command line arguments
     */
    public static void main(String[] args) {
        launch(args);
    }

    @Override
    public void start(Stage primaryStage) {
```

```
        Text text = new Text();
        Button btn = new Button();

        text.setText("Sample Text");
        btn.setText("Button");

        StackPane root = new StackPane();
        root.getChildren().add(btn);
        root.getChildren().add(text);
        primaryStage.setScene(new Scene(root, 300, 250));
        primaryStage.show();
    }
}
```

Notice that the code is using a StackPane as the root in the scene graph. A StackPane arranges its child nodes so that they are "stacked" on top of each other visually. This is done by changing the z-order of each child so that the nodes that are "lower" on the stack have a lower z-order.

Compile and run this app. You can see that if you do not modify the layout of the nodes, they will simply appear jumbled together, as shown in Figure 4-1.

The layout of these nodes is very discordant and does not lend itself to a very usable design. Let's use the HBox layout to organize these nodes on the screen. The HBox belongs to the javafx.scene.layout package. You must import this class before you add the HBox to your Scene:

```
import javafx.scene.layout.HBox;
```

Figure 4-1   Nodes without a layout

After you have imported the correct package, add the HBox to your Scene:

```
HBox root = new HBox();
```

Add all the nodes you want the HBox to hold, just as you would with the StackPanel. The HBox will place all the nodes horizontally within its content.

```
public void start(Stage primaryStage) {
        Text text = new Text();
        Button btn = new Button();

        text.setText("Sample Text");
        btn.setText("Button");

        HBox root = new HBox();
        root.getChildren().add(btn);
        root.getChildren().add(text);
        primaryStage.setScene(new Scene(root, 300, 250));
        primaryStage.show();
    }
```

Notice that you are still not setting the x- and y-coordinate positions of the Text and Button. Under normal circumstances, this would result in the nodes being placed on top of each other. However, the HBox takes care of the placement for you and arranges the nodes neatly next to each other. The full code for your .java file should appear as follows:

```
package Chapter4;

import javafx.application.Application;
import javafx.scene.Scene;
import javafx.scene.control.Button;
import javafx.scene.layout.HBox;
import javafx.scene.text.Text;
import javafx.stage.Stage;

/**
 *
 * @author J F DiMarzio
 */
public class Chapter4 extends Application {

    /**
     * @param args the command line arguments
     */
    public static void main(String[] args) {
        launch(args);
    }
```

```
    @Override
    public void start(Stage primaryStage) {
        Text text = new Text();
        Button btn = new Button();

        text.setText("Sample Text");
        btn.setText("Button");

        HBox root = new HBox();
        root.getChildren().add(btn);
        root.getChildren().add(text);
        primaryStage.setScene(new Scene(root, 300, 250));
        primaryStage.show();
    }
}
```

Compile this app and run it. Your nodes will appear as shown in Figure 4-2.

The HBox layout is simple to use and does not require any parameters to be set to give you great results. It is very easy to line up and organize your nodes using this tool.

Keep in mind that all the layouts in JavaFX, including the HBox, inherit from Node. This means that keyboard and mouse events can be consumed by layouts. Also, you can apply effects to layouts as well, thus giving you a large array of customization options. For more information about using events or effects in nodes, refer to the earlier chapters of this book.

In the next section, you use the VBox to organize your nodes vertically rather than horizontally.

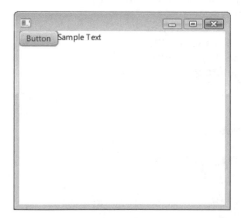

Figure 4-2 Nodes placed using an HBox

The VBox

The VBox is a JavaFX layout that organizes your nodes vertically rather than horizontally like the HBox does. The VBox can be particularly useful in creating forms and other applications where information is generally presented in a top-down manner.

Import the javafx.scene.layout.VBox package to use the VBox layout:

```
import javafx.scene.layout.VBox;
```

The VBox is easy to implement. Add a VBox control to your Scene, as shown in the following code sample:

```
VBox root = new VBox();
```

Using the same Text and Button you used in the previous section's example, let's create a VBox layout. The finished .java file should look like this:

```
package Chapter4;

import javafx.application.Application;
import javafx.scene.Scene;
import javafx.scene.control.Button;
import javafx.scene.layout.VBox;
import javafx.scene.text.Text;
import javafx.stage.Stage;

/**
 *
 * @author J F DiMarzio
 */
public class Chapter4 extends Application {

    /**
     * @param args the command line arguments
     */
    public static void main(String[] args) {
        launch(args);
    }

    @Override
    public void start(Stage primaryStage) {
        Text text = new Text();
        Button btn = new Button();

        text.setText("Sample Text");
        btn.setText("Button");
```

```
        VBox root = new VBox();
        root.getChildren().add(btn);
        root.getChildren().add(text);
        primaryStage.setScene(new Scene(root, 300, 250));
        primaryStage.show();
    }
}
```

Compile and run this app. In the previous section, you used the HBox to organize nodes in a horizontal line. Using the VBox in this app, you can see that the same two nodes now fall under each other vertically. Figure 4-3 shows this result.

Again, this example shows just how easy it is to use a layout in JavaFX to organize your nodes. In the next section, you combine what you have learned so far about layouts to create a nested layout.

Nested Layouts

One of the more flexible aspects of layouts is that they can be nested. That is to say, you can place layouts within each other. You can create some very useful UIs by combining two or more existing layouts.

In the previous sections you looked at two very specific layouts. The HBox only organizes nodes horizontally across a Scene, and a VBox only organizes nodes vertically down a Scene. JavaFX can offer two otherwise limiting layouts and still be versatile because these layouts can be nested within each other to create a more flexible organization of nodes.

Figure 4-3 Organizing nodes using VBox

For example, let's say you want to create a Scene that has a Text node followed by a Button node horizontally. Then, directly under those nodes you want to have another Text node followed by another Button node. This is easily handled by nesting two HBox elements within a VBox.

The VBox organizes nodes vertically. In this case, you want to have two "groups" of nodes arranged vertically. You will have two HBox elements inside the VBox to represent the two horizontal groupings of nodes that are to be stacked on top of each other. Confused? Don't worry, this will become much clearer to you after seeing the code.

To begin, create your VBox instance as follows:

```
VBox root = new VBox();
```

Now, create two separate HBox instances and add them as children to your VBox:

```
HBox row1 = new HBox();
HBox row2 = new HBox();

root.getChildren().add(row1);
root.getChildren().add(row2);
```

These HBox instances give you a place to put the nodes you want to stack. Let's put one Text and one Button in each HBox:

```
Text text1 = new Text();
Button btn1 = new Button();
Text text2 = new Text();
Button btn2 = new Button();

text1.setText("Sample Text 1");
btn1.setText("Button 1");
text2.setText("Sample Text 2");
btn2.setText("Button 2");

VBox root = new VBox();
HBox row1 = new HBox();
HBox row2 = new HBox();

row1.getChildren().add(text1);
row1.getChildren().add(btn1);
row2.getChildren().add(text2);
row2.getChildren().add(btn2);

root.getChildren().add(row1);
root.getChildren().add(row2);
```

That's really all you need to do to nest two different layouts within each other. This process is not limited to just two layouts. Multiple layouts can be nested within each other to produce a more varied layout of nodes. The finished .java file for this example produces a columned effect of two Text and two Button elements. Here is the full code:

```java
package Chapter4;

import javafx.application.Application;
import javafx.scene.Scene;
import javafx.scene.control.Button;
import javafx.scene.layout.HBox;
import javafx.scene.layout.VBox;
import javafx.scene.text.Text;
import javafx.stage.Stage;

/**
 *
 * @author J F DiMarzio
 */
public class Chapter4 extends Application {

    /**
     * @param args the command line arguments
     */
    public static void main(String[] args) {
        launch(args);
    }

    @Override
    public void start(Stage primaryStage) {
        Text text1 = new Text();
        Button btn1 = new Button();
        Text text2 = new Text();
        Button btn2 = new Button();

        text1.setText("Sample Text 1");
        btn1.setText("Button 1");
        text2.setText("Sample Text 2");
        btn2.setText("Button 2");

        VBox root = new VBox();
        HBox row1 = new HBox();
        HBox row2 = new HBox();

        row1.getChildren().add(text1);
        row1.getChildren().add(btn1);
```

Figure 4-4 Nested layout

```
        row2.getChildren().add(text2);
        row2.getChildren().add(btn2);

        root.getChildren().add(row1);
        root.getChildren().add(row2);
        primaryStage.setScene(new Scene(root, 300, 250));
        primaryStage.show();
    }
}
```

Compile and run this app. You will see the layout shown in Figure 4-4.

Now you can experiment with the other layouts. Try to nest these layouts to produce custom ones that are original and engaging.

Try This Using Other Layouts

Using the examples given in this chapter, create a JavaFX application that uses a FlowPane, GridPane, or TilePane layout to display three images. Notice how each layout changes the display of the images.

In the next chapter, you will draw shapes to the screen.

Chapter 4 Self Test

1. What layout organizes your nodes horizontally across a Scene?

2. True or false? The HBox is located in the javafx.scene package.

3. What property holds the nodes for a layout to organize?

4. True or false? You must be sure to set the x- and y-coordinates of each node you place in a layout.

5. Can effects be applied to layouts?

6. What layout organizes nodes vertically down a Scene?

7. What is the name given to layouts that are combined to produce a new layout?

8. True or false? For layouts to be nested, one must inherit from the other.

9. True or false? Only two layouts can be nested.

10. Name three layouts other than VBox and HBox.

Chapter 5
Creating Shapes

Key Skills & Concepts

- Drawing lines to the screen

- Working with the context menu

- Creating complex shapes

In this chapter, you learn how to draw shapes to the screen. Shapes add interest and dimension to your applications. You will start by learning how to draw a basic line. From there, you will move on to rectilinear shapes. From these basic rectilinear shapes, you will move on to polygons and curvilinear shapes.

NOTE

If you are interested in game development or other animation-based media, polygons are very important. Polygons create the base of most 3-D objects.

Before you start drawing shapes, you need to take a second and learn about the JavaFX scene graph and exactly what it does for your applications.

JavaFX Scene Graph

The JavaFX scene graph API controls how and when objects are drawn to the screen in your application. In the past—and even with some frameworks today—you had to be acutely aware of what needed to be drawn to the screen and when. You would need to invalidate and redraw the parts of the screen that have changed. JavaFX takes care of this for you.

The JavaFX scene graph is a specialized API that holds and tracks a model of the objects you place on your GUI. That is, let's say you want to draw a square to the screen; the screen graph will hold that square and all the information about its surrounding objects, drawing them and redrawing them as needed. How does the screen graph do this?

The scene graph is a tree-style container that contains nodes. There are three kinds of nodes within the scene graph. The base node of the scene graph—the node that will hold all of the other nodes—is a *root* node. Roots have no parent nodes and can contain children. There are also branch nodes and leaf nodes. Branch nodes can also contain other child node types. Leaf nodes, however, can hold no child nodes. A square, a Text, and a Button are all leaf nodes. They can be placed on the root or a branch, but can contain no other child nodes. A VBox, on the other hand, can be a branch in that it can be placed on the root and can hold other child nodes.

Now that you understand what the scene graph is, let's draw some shapes.

Drawing Shapes

You will be drawing shapes on your application, in this chapter, without the help of the JavaFX Scene Builder. The JavaFX Scene Builder is a great tool, and it can be extremely handy when you need some quick code. The problem is that if you rely too heavily on this automatically produced code, you will not learn how to create these nodes on your own. The goal in learning a new language is to gain the knowledge needed to write code. However, if you only rely on automated, drag and-drop code, you really will not learn that much.

In the following six sections, you will begin drawing lines to the screen. As you move through these sections, you will start to create more complicated shapes, including polygons and ellipses. Finally, you will draw pre-rendered images to the screen before moving on to applying effects.

Before You Begin

First off, you need to prepare your project. All the lessons in this chapter can be done in a single JavaFX application project. Create a new JavaFX application (using the new JavaFX application template) and name it **Chapter5**.

Once the projected is created, open the Chapter5.java file and delete the following lines of code; they are used to create a Hello World application:

```
import javafx.event.ActionEvent;
import javafx.event.EventHandler;
import javafx.scene.control.Button;

primaryStage.setTitle("Hello World!");
Button btn = new Button();
btn.setText("Say 'Hello World'");
btn.setOnAction(new EventHandler<ActionEvent>() {
    @Override
    public void handle(ActionEvent event) {
    System.out.println("Hello World!");
    }
});
...
root.getChildren().add(btn);
```

Before continuing with this chapter, ensure the code in your Chapter5.java file looks like this:

```
package Chapter5;

import javafx.application.Application;
import javafx.scene.Scene;
import javafx.scene.layout.StackPane;
import javafx.stage.Stage;

/**
 *
 * @author J F DiMarzio
 */
public class Chapter5 extends Application {

    /**
     * @param args the command line arguments
     */
    public static void main(String[] args) {
        launch(args);
    }

    @Override
    public void start(Stage primaryStage) {

        StackPane root = new StackPane();
        primaryStage.setScene(new Scene(root, 300, 250));
        primaryStage.show();
    }
}
```

Lines

A line is the most basic form of a shape. Almost any shape you can think of, draw, or create is made up of one or more lines. From squares and triangles, as collections of straight lines, to circles and ellipses, as collections of curved lines, understanding the basics of line drawing is crucial. Given that almost all the other shapes you will draw are based on the line, it seems logical to begin this chapter learning about lines.

What is a line? This may seem like an elementary question. We have all been drawing lines on paper, with pencils, crayons, and markers, since our earliest school days. You can use that experience of drawing lines on paper with a crayon to understand what a "line" is in JavaFX.

When you draw a line on a piece of paper, you place your crayon down on one point, drag it across to another point, and lift up the crayon. The line you draw is as thick as the crayon you used to draw it. The line is also the same color as the crayon. This same logic can be applied to drawing a line in JavaFX.

When you draw a line in JavaFX, you must tell the compiler the start and end points of your line. The values you need to specify are the starting X and starting Y as well as the ending X and ending Y. The compiler will be able to take this information and draw a line on the screen between these two points.

NOTE
The start and end points are expressed using the Cartesian coordinate system.

You must start by specifying an import statement in your code. The import statement you need references the code for drawing lines. The package for lines is required for the compiler to understand what your code is trying to do as well as to draw a line accordingly.

At the top of your Chapter5.java file, under the existing import statements, include the following statement:

```
import javafx.scene.shape.Line;
```

Next, within the start() method, instantiate a new Line node as follows:

```
Line line = new Line();
```

Now you can set the starting and ending x- and y-coordinates. After you instantiate the Line node, type in **line.**, as shown here:

```
line.
```

When you do, a context menu should appear. If the context menu does not automatically appear, press CRTL-SPACEBAR. This keystroke shortcut will bring up the context menu shown in Figure 5-1.

The context menu is an invaluable tool that shows you all the options available to you from a specific place in your script. The context menu can be used to discover elements or attributes that you otherwise would not be aware of. The context menu can even be used to see some of the values that can be assigned to attributes. You should commit the CRTL-SPACEBAR keystroke shortcut to memory because you will find yourself using it quite often.

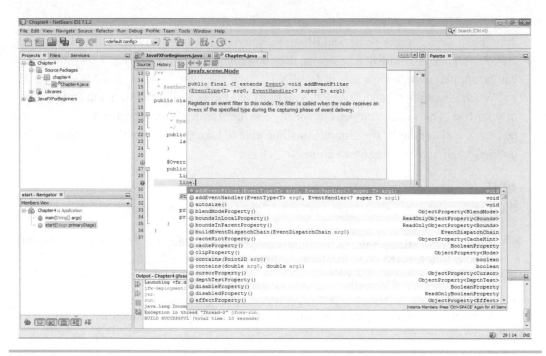

Figure 5-1 Context menu

If you press the ENTER key while the context menu is on a property or method, as shown in Figure 5-1, that property or method will be inserted into your code.

Scroll through your context menu, or begin typing, until you see setStartX. The startX attribute is one of the four attributes you need to specify in order to draw the line. Make sure the setStartX method is highlighted, and then press the ENTER key.

Pass the setStartX method a value of 10. Each line of code in a Java file ends with a semicolon (with some exceptions). Use the ENTER key to move to a new line after each line of code. Next, use the context menu to insert a call to setStartY and assign it a value of 10 as well.

You will be drawing a line that extends from x10, y10 to x150, y150. Seeing as you have just assigned 10,10 to the starting X and starting Y, use the context menu to finish assigning the correct values to the ending X and ending Y. Your code should look like this:

```
package Chapter5;

import javafx.application.Application;
import javafx.scene.Scene;
import javafx.scene.layout.StackPane;
```

```
import javafx.scene.shape.Line;
import javafx.stage.Stage;

/**
 *
 * @author J F DiMarzio
 */
public class Chapter5 extends Application {
    /**
     * @param args the command line arguments
     */
    public static void main(String[] args) {
        launch(args);
    }
@Override
    public void start(Stage primaryStage) {
        Line line = new Line();
        line.setStartX(10);
        line.setStartY(10);
        line.setEndX(150);
        line.setEndY(150);
        StackPane root = new StackPane();

        primaryStage.setScene(new Scene(root, 300, 250));
        primaryStage.show();
    }
}
```

Notice in this code that there is an existing instantiation of a StackPane called root. To get your line onto the application UI, you need to add it as a child to this StackPane. Insert the following line of code after the instantiation of the StackPane:

```
root.getChildren().add(line);
```

This line of code adds the Line node that you created to the children collection of the application's StackPane. Run your application, and you should get a line that looks like the one shown in Figure 5-2.

This looks like a great line, and you should be very proud of the job you have done—but all things considered, it is not very exciting. You can assign a few more property values to this line to make it a little more interesting. The discussion that follows details some the properties available to the Line node.

To begin, to make your line a little thicker, use the strokeWidth property. The strokeWidth property does exactly what the name implies—it governs the thickness or width of the Line node. Use the setStringWidth() method of the Line node to assign the strokeWidth property a value of 15. This will make your line stand out a bit more.

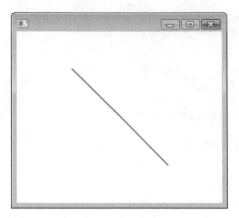

Figure 5-2 A line

Adding some color to your line will make it pop out even more. Color is a common attribute for shapes. To work with color, you need to import the javafx.scene.paint.Color package. Therefore, add the following import statement to your file:

```
line.setStroke(Color.TOMATO);
```

To color the Line node a nice shade of tomato red, use the setStroke() method to assign the stroke property a value of Color.TOMATO. The stroke property acts just like the stroke of a paint brush. It can contain information about color, gradients, and other visually appealing details of a shape. Here's the code for setting the stroke property:

```
stroke : Color.TOMATO
```

Your new Line node should have the following calls:

```
Line line = new Line();
line.setStartX(10);
line.setStartY(10);
line.setEndX(150);
line.setEndY(150);
line.setStrokeWidth(15);
line.setStroke(Color.TOMATO);
```

Run your application, and you will see a nice red line from the upper left to the lower right of the screen.

The previous line can also be created using the LineBuilder class, which can be used to make your code much more concise. You should use the Builder classes wherever possible in your code, as follows:

```
lineBuilder.create().startX(10).startY(10).endX(150)
                    .endY(150).stroke(Color.TOMATO)
                    .strokeWidth(15).build();
```

Let's draw three of these lines to form the shape of the letter *U*. Try to lay out the three lines on your own. The first line should run down the left side of the screen. The second line should run from the end of the first line, across the bottom, to the right side of the screen. Finally, the third line should run from the end of the bottom line to the top on the right side of the screen.

NOTE
Before you begin, change the StackPane to an AnchorPane and add the correct import for it; otherwise, you may get some unwanted results. An explanation as to why will come later in the book.

When you are finished, compare your code to the code that follows:

```
package Chapter5;

import javafx.application.Application;
import javafx.scene.Scene;
import javafx.scene.layout.AnchorPane;
import javafx.scene.paint.Color;
import javafx.scene.shape.Line;
import javafx.stage.Stage;

/**
 *
 * @author J F DiMarzio
 */
public class Chapter5 extends Application {
    /**
     * @param args the command line arguments
     */
    public static void main(String[] args) {
        launch(args);
    }
    @Override
    public void start(Stage primaryStage) {
        Line line1 = new Line();
        Line line2 = new Line();
        Line line3 = new Line();
```

```
line1.setStartX(10);
line1.setStartY(10);
line1.setEndX(10);
line1.setEndY(100);
line1.setStrokeWidth(15);
line1.setStroke(Color.TOMATO);

line2.setStartX(10);
line2.setStartY(100);
line2.setEndX(100);
line2.setEndY(100);
line2.setStrokeWidth(15);
line2.setStroke(Color.TOMATO);

line3.setStartX(100);
line3.setStartY(100);
line3.setEndX(100);
line3.setEndY(10);
line3.setStrokeWidth(15);
line3.setStroke(Color.TOMATO);

AnchorPane root = new AnchorPane();

root.getChildren().add(line1);
root.getChildren().add(line2);
root.getChildren().add(line3);

primaryStage.setScene(new Scene(root, 300, 250));
primaryStage.show();
    }
}
```

Run your code and compare the results to those shown in Figure 5-3.

Drawing separate lines for every shape and configuration you can think of is not a very economic use of your time as a developer. Just imagine what it would be like if you had to draw every line, one at a time, to form simple shapes. Luckily there is another type of line you can use called a polyline. It lets you specify more than one set of points in one line, the last of which are the end points. Specifying more than one end point lets you draw more complex lines with less code. Let's try to draw the same U-shaped, three-line configuration using a Polyline node.

The first step to using a Polyline node is to import the Polyline package. The code for using polylines is different from the code for lines. For this reason, you need to import a separate class to work with polylines:

```
import javafx.scene.shape.Polyline;
```

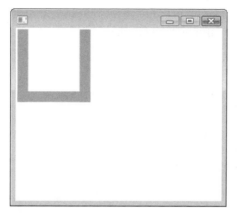

Figure 5-3 Three lines

With the package imported, instantiate a new Polyline. Bring up the context menu to view the available methods.

Notice that there are no methods for setStartX and setStartY. Rather, a Polyline accepts an array of points. The getPoints() method returns an ObservableList of all the points that make up your Polyline. One of the methods of an ObservableList is add(). Therefore, you can use the add() method of getPoints() to add a new array of points.

When you're passing an array of points to a Polyline node, it is understood that the first two values will be the x- and y-coordinates of the start point, and the last two will be the end point. The Polyline class will instinctively draw your line between these points, stopping at all other points in your array. You can easily replicate the "U" formation of lines you created with Line using an array of points in Polyline.

An array of points that will match the points used in the Line example should look like this:

```
new Double[]{10.0, 10.0,
             10.0, 100.0,
             100.0, 100.0,
             100.0, 10.0 }
```

Note that each value in the array is separated by a comma.

TIP

To keep the array visually easy to understand, you can separate each x,y pair onto a new line. Whitespace within an array will be ignored by the compiler and can be added to make your array easy to read.

Run the following code. It should produce the same three-lined U shape as the previous example—but with much less code:

```java
package Chapter5;

import javafx.application.Application;
import javafx.scene.Scene;
import javafx.scene.layout.AnchorPane;
import javafx.scene.paint.Color;
import javafx.scene.shape.Polyline;
import javafx.stage.Stage;

/**
 *
 * @author J F DiMarzio
 */
public class Chapter5 extends Application {

    /**
     * @param args the command line arguments
     */
    public static void main(String[] args) {
        launch(args);
    }

    @Override
    public void start(Stage primaryStage) {
        Polyline polyline = new Polyline();

        polyline.getPoints().addAll(new Double[]{
            10.0, 10.0,
            10.0, 100.0,
            100.0, 100.0,
            100.0, 10.0 });
        polyline.setStrokeWidth(15);
        polyline.setStroke(Color.TOMATO);

        AnchorPane root = new AnchorPane();
        root.getChildren().add(polyline);

        primaryStage.setScene(new Scene(root, 300, 250));
        primaryStage.show();
    }
}
```

With this section complete, you have learned how to create simple lines and draw them to the screen. In the next section, you start to apply some of the knowledge you have picked up thus far and begin to create more complex shapes such as rectilinear and curvilinear objects.

Rectangles

The JavaFX Rectangle node is used to refer to either a square or rectangle. It is used to draw any parallel-lined, four-sided shape. Given that the only difference between rectangles and squares is the length of a set of sides, it only makes sense that the same element can be used to draw either shape.

In the previous section you learned that a Polyline takes an array of points to create a multilined shape. The Rectangle refines this process by only requiring one point be specified. When you create a rectangle, you only need to specify the point for the upper-left corner of the shape. This point, when combined with a defined width and height, will give you a finished shape.

The code that is needed to create rectangles is contained within a package separate from that of the core JavaFX code. You will need to import the javafx.scene.shape.Rectangle class before you can create a rectangle. Therefore, insert the following import statements into your file:

```
import javafx.scene.shape.Rectangle;
```

You are going to draw a rectangle that starts at the point x10, y10. It will be 100 pixels wide and 150 pixels high.

NOTE
Do not get confused by the term *height*. The height of a rectangle is actually calculated from the start point, down (not the start point, up, as the name might imply). Therefore, a rectangle that starts at the point 1,1 and has a height of 100 will extend 100 pixels down from the point 1,1.

You will be specifying seven properties for the Rectangle element:

- **x**   The x-coordinate for the upper-left corner of the rectangle

- **y**   The y-coordinate for the upper-left corner of the rectangle

- **width**   The width of the rectangle

- **height**   The height of the rectangle

- **fill**   The color of the interior area of the rectangle

- **stroke**   The attributes of the lines used to draw the rectangle

- **strokeWidth**   The size of the line used to draw the rectangle

The first four attributes, shown next, are self-explanatory and their values are easy to determine:

```
Rectangle rectangle = new Rectangle();
rectangle.setX(10);
rectangle.setY(10);
rectangle.setWidth(100);
rectangle.setHeight(150);
```

The remaining three attributes may require a little explanation. All basic shapes, with the exceptions of lines and polylines, are filled in with Color.BLACK by default. For the purposes of the example you are building here, you only want to have the lines of the rectangle visible. Therefore, to have the rectangle not be filled with color and only expose the lines that create its border, you have to explicitly set the fill property to null.

Finally, the stroke and the strokeWidth properties will be set just as they were in the previous section. That is, set the stroke to Color.BLACK and the strokeWidth to 5. Keep in mind, the stroke and strokeWidth only refer to the lines of the rectangle, not the inner area of the rectangle.

Your finished Rectangle code should look like this:

```
@Override
public void start(Stage primaryStage) {
    Rectangle rectangle = new Rectangle();

    rectangle.setX(10);
    rectangle.setY(10);
    rectangle.setWidth(100);
    rectangle.setHeight(150);
    rectangle.setFill(null);
    rectangle.setStroke(Color.BLACK);
    rectangle.setStrokeWidth(5);

    AnchorPane root = new AnchorPane();
    root.getChildren().add(rectangle);

    primaryStage.setScene(new Scene(root, 300, 250));
    primaryStage.show();
}
```

You can also use the RectangleBuilder in much the same way you used the LineBuilder to create this same shape, as follows. In short, you should use these JavaFX Builder classes to make your life much easier, wherever you can in your code.

```
rectangleBuilder.create().x(10).y(10)
                .width(100).height(150).stroke(Color.Black)
                .strokeWidth(5).build();
```

TIP

To see what the rectangle looks like filled in, remove the fill attribute or set it to a specific color.

Notice that the line color is governed by the stoke attribute, whereas the interior color is governed by the fill attribute. This means that you can have a rectangle with a line color that's different from the fill color. Here's an example:

```
@Override
public void start(Stage primaryStage) {
    Rectangle rectangle = new Rectangle();

    rectangle.setX(10);
    rectangle.setY(10);
    rectangle.setWidth(100);
    rectangle.setHeight(150);
    rectangle.setFill(Color.BLUE);
    rectangle.setStroke(Color.RED);
    rectangle.setStrokeWidth(5);

    AnchorPane root = new AnchorPane();
    root.getChildren().add(rectangle);

    primaryStage.setScene(new Scene(root, 300, 250));
    primaryStage.show();
}
```

Two more interesting attributes of the Rectangle element are worth noting. If you want to round out the corners of your rectangle, you can use the attributes arcWidth and arcHeight to control the rounding. The attributes arcWidth and arcHeight are used to define the amount of arc that is used when rounding the corners of the rectangle.

The arcWidth and arcHeight attributes are not available to Line and Polyline because this would basically turn the lines and polylines into arcs. Arcs are covered a bit later in this chapter.

Try the following code to round the corners of your rectangle:

```
@Override
public void start(Stage primaryStage) {
    Rectangle rectangle = new Rectangle();

    rectangle.setX(10);
    rectangle.setY(10);
    rectangle.setWidth(100);
    rectangle.setHeight(150);
```

```
    rectangle.setFill(null);
    rectangle.setStroke(Color.BLACK);
    rectangle.setStrokeWidth(5);
    rectangle.setArcHeight(20);
    rectangle.setArcWidth(20);

    AnchorPane root = new AnchorPane();
    root.getChildren().add(rectangle);

    primaryStage.setScene(new Scene(root, 300, 250));
    primaryStage.show();
}
```

Now that you have learned how to draw a rectangle on the screen, you can move on to a more complex shape—the polygon. The next section discusses the process for drawing polygons, or multisided shapes, to the screen using JavaFX.

Polygons

A polygon is to a rectangle what the polyline is to the line. Polygon nodes are set up similarly to Polyline (discussed in a previous section of this chapter). Whereas Line and Rectangle accept a fixed number of coordinates to use a point, Polyline and Polygon accept an array of points.

Polygons will draw lines between all the points you specify in your points array, the same way Polyline does.

NOTE
The same rules about color that apply to Rectangle nodes also apply to Polygon nodes. By default, all polygons are filled with black. Also, the line color and fill color are governed by the stroke and fill attributes, respectively.

The following sample code draws a simple, small octagon on the screen using the Polygon element:

```
package Chapter5;

import javafx.application.Application;
import javafx.scene.Scene;
import javafx.scene.layout.AnchorPane;
import javafx.scene.shape.Polygon;
import javafx.stage.Stage;

/**
 *
 * @author J F DiMarzio
```

```
 */
public class Chapter5 extends Application {

    /**
     * @param args the command line arguments
     */
    public static void main(String[] args) {
        launch(args);
    }

    @Override
    public void start(Stage primaryStage) {
        Polygon polygon = new Polygon();

        polygon.getPoints().addAll(new Double[]{
                90.0,80.0,
                190.0,80.0,
                240.0,130.0,
                240.0,220.0,
                190.0,270.0,
                90.0,270.0,
                40.0,220.0,
                40.0,130.0
        });

        AnchorPane root = new AnchorPane();
        root.getChildren().add(polygon);

        primaryStage.setScene(new Scene(root, 300, 250));
        primaryStage.show();
    }
}
```

Notice that you do not need to specify the final point of the polygon as being the same as the first point. JavaFX will automatically know that it should connect the last point in your array with the first point to complete the shape.

In the next section of this chapter, you learn how to create curvilinear shapes such as arcs, circles, and ellipses.

Arcs

Although on the surface an arc may seem like a simple shape, it can be very complicated for a computer to understand. People look at an arc and think, "It's just a piece of a circle." To a computer, an arc is composed of complex radius and center points, angles, and circumference lengths.

An Arc element takes seven basic attributes. Given the complexity of drawing an arc as opposed to drawing a straight line, the attributes needed to complete an arc are unlike those you have seen so far in this chapter and therefore need some explanation. To begin, import the following classes:

```
import javafx.scene.shape.Arc;
import javafx.scene.shape.ArcType;
```

The first two required attributes are centerX and centerY:

```
arc.setCenterX(125);
arc.setCenterY(125);
```

Think of a circle for a moment. An arc would be a segment of that circle. JavaFX thinks of an arc as a circle that it only has to draw part of. Therefore, the centerX and centerY attributes represent the center point of the circle that the arc would form if it was completed.

The next two attributes are radiusX and radiusY:

```
arc.setRadiusX(50);
arc.setRadiusY(50);
```

Every circle extends a certain distance from its center. This distance is the radius. The Arc node requires that you specify a radius. However, the naming of the property may be a little misleading, because radiusX and radiusY do not represent a point. Rather, they represent the radius in length along the x- and y-axes. Having two separate radial lengths lets you create oblong arcs.

TIP

To make a circular arc, set the radiusX and radiusY properties to the same value.

The next required attribute is startAngle:

```
arc.setStartAngle(45);
```

The startAngle represents an invisible line that extends from your center point to the actual start point of your arc. This line is at a given angle. Therefore, a startAngle of 45 means that the arc will begin at a 45-degree angle to the center point.

The next attribute required to create an arc is the length:

```
arc.setLength(270);
```

The other length-related properties you have worked with thus far, such as width and height, have been based on pixel length. The Arc property of length is a representation of the number of degrees that the arc travels from its start point. Therefore, if you have a length with a value of 270, your arc will extend 270 degrees from the start point, around the center point.

The next Arc attribute is type:

```
arc.setType(ArcType.OPEN);
```

The type property of the Arc element describes how the arc is drawn. Three different ArcType values can be assigned to this property:

- **ArcType.OPEN**   Draws the arc as an open-ended curved line
- **ArcType.ROUND**   Draws the arc while connecting the two end points back to the center point, much like a pie with a piece missing
- **ArcType.CHORD**   Draws the arc and then connects the two end points to each other with a straight line

The last properties you need to set are the fill and stroke. The fill attribute is the same for an Arc element as it is for other shape elements. For the purposes of this example, set the fill attribute to null.

Set the stroke to Color.BLACK, as you have done in the past sections. Run the code that follows to create an arc that looks like a pie with a missing piece:

```
package Chapter5;

import javafx.application.Application;
import javafx.scene.Scene;
import javafx.scene.layout.AnchorPane;
import javafx.scene.paint.Color;
import javafx.scene.shape.Arc;
import javafx.scene.shape.ArcType;
import javafx.stage.Stage;

/**
 *
 * @author J F DiMarzio
 */
public class Chapter5 extends Application {

    /**
     * @param args the command line arguments
     */
```

```
    public static void main(String[] args) {
        launch(args);
    }

    @Override
    public void start(Stage primaryStage) {
        Arc arc = new Arc();

        arc.setCenterX(125);
        arc.setCenterY(125);
        arc.setRadiusX(50);
        arc.setRadiusY(50);
        arc.setStartAngle(45);
        arc.setLength(270);
        arc.setType(ArcType.OPEN);
        arc.setFill(null);
        arc.setStroke(Color.BLACK);

        AnchorPane root = new AnchorPane();
        root.getChildren().add(arc);

        primaryStage.setScene(new Scene(root, 300, 250));
        primaryStage.show();
    }
}
```

Although it requires the use of several properties that may seem foreign to you, creating arcs becomes easier as you understand the purpose of each property.

Again, JavaFX provides another Builder class to make this process much easier. The ArcBuilder can be used as follows:

```
arcBuilder.create().centerX(125).centerY(125)
                   .radiusX(50).radiusY(50).startAngle(45)
                   .length(270).type(ArcType.OPEN)
                   .stroke(Color,BLACK).build();
```

In the next section, you will create circles and ellipses.

Circles and Ellipses

Creating a circle using JavaFX will seem much easier after you have created an arc. Whereas an Arc node needs seven attributes to govern angles, lengths, and other features, a Circle node only requires three. But before you can create a circle, you must import the appropriate package:

```
import javafx.scene.shape.Circle;
```

The three properties required to create a circle are centerX, centerY, and radius. These attributes function exactly like they do for an arc.

NOTE

A Circle node only has a single value for the radius and not a height and width pair for the radius, like Arc, because a circle cannot be "oblong." Therefore, it will always have the same radial value along all axes.

Having a simple set of attributes makes circles easy to create and use in your applications. The following code creates a black outline of a circle:

```java
package Chapter5;

import javafx.application.Application;
import javafx.scene.Scene;
import javafx.scene.layout.AnchorPane;
import javafx.scene.paint.Color;
import javafx.scene.shape.Circle;
import javafx.stage.Stage;

/**
 *
 * @author J F DiMarzio
 */
public class Chapter5 extends Application {

    /**
     * @param args the command line arguments
     */
    public static void main(String[] args) {
        launch(args);
    }

    @Override
    public void start(Stage primaryStage) {
        Circle circle = new Circle();

        circle.setCenterX(125);
        circle.setCenterY(125);
        circle.setRadius(50);
        circle.setFill(null);
        circle.setStroke(Color.BLACK);

        AnchorPane root = new AnchorPane();
        root.getChildren().add(circle);
```

```
        primaryStage.setScene(new Scene(root, 300, 250));
        primaryStage.show();
    }
}
```

You can use this same process to create an ellipse. The only difference between an ellipse and a circle is that because an ellipse is oblong, the Ellipse element takes an x, y radial pair rather than a set radial length. Here's the code:

```
package Chapter5;

import javafx.application.Application;
import javafx.scene.Scene;
import javafx.scene.layout.AnchorPane;
import javafx.scene.paint.Color;
import javafx.scene.shape.Ellipse;
import javafx.stage.Stage;

/**
 *
 * @author J F DiMarzio
 */
public class Chapter5 extends Application {

    /**
     * @param args the command line arguments
     */
    public static void main(String[] args) {
        launch(args);
    }

    @Override
    public void start(Stage primaryStage) {
        Ellipse ellipse = new Ellipse();

        ellipse.setCenterX(125);
        ellipse.setCenterY(125);
        ellipse.setRadiusX(35);
        ellipse.setRadiusY(20);
        ellipse.setFill(null);
        ellipse.setStroke(Color.BLACK);

        AnchorPane root = new AnchorPane();
        root.getChildren().add(ellipse);

        primaryStage.setScene(new Scene(root, 300, 250));
        primaryStage.show();
    }
}
```

Try This Create Multiple Shapes

Take some time out before the next chapter to exercise your new shape-building skills. Although it may seem like a fairly elementary task, you will have a great need to create simple shapes throughout your development career. From designing new buttons, to creating masks, you will always need to create simple shapes.

Try adding multiple shapes to the same Scene. Play with the dimensions and positions of the shapes to keep them from overlapping. Continue to work with them to manipulate how the shapes can touch or cover each other.

This exercise will be useful in future development by giving you a full grasp of how elements are placed in a Scene.

In this chapter, you learned how to create some basic shapes without using the JavaFX Scene Builder. You created lines, polylines, rectangles, arcs, circles, and ellipses. You also learned about an invaluable tool: the context menu. These skills will help you tremendously throughout the remainder of this book.

In the next chapter, you will learn how to work with and create more colors than what was touched on in this chapter. You will also learn how to apply effects such as opacity and rotation.

Chapter 5 Self Test

1. What four properties are needed to draw a line?
2. How do you access the context menu?
3. What package is needed when working with colors?
4. What property controls the thickness of the line used to draw a shape?
5. What package is needed to draw a polyline?
6. What type of value is assigned to the points property of a Polyline node?
7. True or false? The height property of the Rectangle node is the number of pixels from the start point to the top of the rectangle.
8. What is the default value for the fill property of a Rectangle node?
9. True or false? RadiusX and radiusY comprise the point where the radius extends to.
10. What property configures the radius of a circle?

Chapter 6
Using Colors
and Gradients

Key Skills & Concepts

- Creating mixed colors
- Applying colors to shapes
- Using gradients

In this chapter, you explore more deeply the powerful coloring and gradient tools available to you in JavaFX. In Chapter 5 you learned how to apply some basic, pre-created colors to shapes. In this chapter you learn how to mix your own colors, and you apply these colors to shapes and use them in gradients.

Using Color

The Color class is a very powerful class. In the last chapter you used a very small part of the Color class to fill a Line node with a solid color. You used just one or two of the 148 predefined colors of the Color class. This is a small sample of what the Color class is capable of.

The Color class can be used four different ways, each providing a capable method for creating the colors you need for any situation. You can invoke the Color class to use predefined colors, RGB values, HSB values, or web hex values.

In this section you learn more about the predefined colors available to you as well as the other color methods.

Predefined Colors

The Color class, as contained in the javafx.scene.paint.Color package, has a number of predefined colors you can use instantly in the attributes of your nodes. In the previous chapter you used a predefined color (Color.TOMATO) to fill a line. In fact, all shapes use the Color.BLACK predefined color as the fill. The Color class provides the following predefined colors:

ALICEBLUE	ANTIQUEWHITE	AQUA
AQUAMARINE	AZURE	BEIGE
BISQUE	BLACK	BLANCHEDALMOND
BLUE	BLUEVIOLET	BROWN
BURLYWOOD	CADETBLUE	CHARTREUSE

CHOCOLATE	CORAL	CORNFLOWERBLUE
CORNSILK	CRIMSON	CYAN
DARKBLUE	DARKCYAN	DARKGOLDENROD
DARKGRAY	DARKGREEN	DARKGREY
DARKKHAKI	DARKMAGENTA	DARKOLIVEGREEN
DARKORANGE	DARKORCHID	DARKRED
DARKSALMON	DARKSEAGREEN	DARKSLATEBLUE
DARKSLATEGRAY	DARKSLATEGREY	DARKTURQUOISE
DARKVIOLET	DEEPPINK	DEEPSKYBLUE
DIMGRAY	DIMGREY	DODGERBLUE
FIREBRICK	FLORALWHITE	FORESTGREEN
FUCHSIA	GAINSBORO	GHOSTWHITE
GOLD	GOLDENROD	GRAY
GREEN	GREENYELLOW	GREY
HONEYDEW	HOTPINK	INDIANRED
INDIGO	IVORY	KHAKI
LAVENDER	LAVENDERBLUSH	LAWNGREEN
LEMONCHIFFON	LIGHTBLUE	LIGHTCORAL
LIGHTCYAN	LIGHTGOLDENRODYELLOW	LIGHTGRAY
LIGHTGREEN	LIGHTGREY	LIGHTPINK
LIGHTSALMON	LIGHTSEAGREEN	LIGHTSKYBLUE
LIGHTSLATEGRAY	LIGHTSLATEGREY	LIGHTSTEELBLUE
LIGHTYELLOW	LIME	LIMEGREEN
LINEN	MAGENTA	MAROON
MEDIUMAQUAMARINE	MEDIUMBLUE	MEDIUMORCHID
MEDIUMPURPLE	MEDIUMSEAGREEN	MEDIUMSLATEBLUE
MEDIUMSPRINGGREEN	MEDIUMTURQUOISE	MEDIUMVIOLETRED
MIDNIGHTBLUE	MINTCREAM	MISTYROSE
MOCCASIN	NAVAJOWHITE	NAVY
OLDLACE	OLIVE	OLIVEDRAB
ORANGE	ORANGERED	ORCHID
PALEGOLDENROD	PALEGREEN	PALETURQUOISE
PALEVIOLETRED	PAPAYAWHIP	PEACHPUFF

PERU	PINK	PLUM
POWDERBLUE	PURPLE	RED
ROSYBROWN	ROYALBLUE	SADDLEBROWN
SALMON	SANDYBROWN	SEAGREEN
SEASHELL	SIENNA	SILVER
SKYBLUE	SLATEBLUE	SLATEGRAY
SLATEGREY	SNOW	SPRINGGREEN
STEELBLUE	TAN	TEAL
THISTLE	TOMATO	TRANSPARENT
TURQUOISE	VIOLET	WHEAT
WHITE	WHITESMOKE	YELLOW
YELLOWGREEN		

A predefined color is accessed as a constant of the Color class. For example, in the Color class, the constant BLUE is associated with the values needed to create the blue color. Let's take a look at the following line of code (which is associated with a shape):

```
ellipse.setFill(Color.BLUE);
```

When you assign the fill attribute a value of Color.BLUE, the Color class passes along the values needed to create a blue color.

The Color class does offer a vast array of predefined colors to use in your scripts. But what if one of the predefined colors does not quite fit what you need? Fear not—the Color class has an even more powerful set of methods for rendering almost any color you could possibly need.

Next, you learn about the methods available in the Color class for creating colors that are not predefined.

Mixing Colors

If you have looked at the predefined colors but cannot find the exact one you need, you can always mix or specify your own color. The Color class would be a very limited tool if you could only use predefined colors without the ability to customize them.

For this reason, the Color class has three useful methods for mixing your own colors:

```
Color.rgb();
Color.hsb();
Color.web();
```

Let's look at each of these methods and how to use them.

Color.rgb

The Color class allows you to use the RGB (Red, Green, Blue) value of the color you want to create. Most colors are mixed as a composite of differing amounts of red, green, and blue. The amounts of red, green, and blue used to create a color are defined using a value from 0 to 255 (0 being none of that color, 255 being a full amount of the specified color). The following code will fill the interior of a rectangle with purple:

```
Rectangle rectangle = new Rectangle();
rectangle.setX(10);
rectangle.setY(10);
rectangle.setHeight(150);

rectangle.setWidth(150);
rectangle.setFill(Color.rgb(255, 0, 255));
```

In this method call to the Color class, you specify an RGB value of 255 red, 0 green, and 255 blue. This produces a purple color. However, try the following code and see what you get:

```
Rectangle rectangle = new Rectangle();
Color purple = new Color(1,0,1,1);
rectangle.setX(10);
rectangle.setY(10);
rectangle.setHeight(150);
rectangle.setWidth(150);
rectangle.setFill(purple);
```

This code also produces a rectangle that is filled with purple. The default constructor for the Color class also accepts RGB values to create a color. So what is the difference? The end result is the same either way: You are left with purple as the color. The difference is that the default constructor for the Color class accepts values for red, green, and blue as a float from 0 to 1. Keep in mind that the rgb method of the Color class accepts values from 0 to 255. The final value is Alpha, which should be 1 to be fully opaque.

Color.hsb

The Color class also has a method for HSB (Hue, Saturation, Brightness) colors. In the HSB color model, the color or hue is represented by a number from 0 to 360. This number corresponds to one of the 360 degrees of a color wheel.

The saturation and brightness attributes are represented by a number from 0 to 1. A value of 0 is no saturation and no brightness, whereas a value of 1 is full saturation and full brightness. To create the same purple color you just created with the rgb method, use the following code:

```
Rectangle rectangle = new Rectangle();

rectangle.setX(10);
rectangle.setY(10);
rectangle.setHeight(150);
rectangle.setWidth(150);
rectangle.setFill(Color.hsb(300,1,1));
```

Color.web

Finally, the Color class can also use a web color hex value to create a color for you. The web method of the Color class accepts a standard hex value. Here's an example:

```
Rectangle rectangle = new Rectangle();

rectangle.setX(10);
rectangle.setY(10);
rectangle.setHeight(150);
rectangle.setWidth(150);
rectangle.setFill(Color.web("#FF00FF"));
```

The alpha Attribute

One last attribute of the Color class you should take note of is the alpha attribute. Every method of the Color class has an optional alpha attribute. The alpha value controls the opacity of the color being created. The alpha is a value between 0 and 1, where 0 is transparent and 1 is opaque. The alpha value can be added to any of the methods of the Color class.

By setting the alpha value to 0, you will achieve full transparency:

```
Rectangle rectangle = new Rectangle();

rectangle.setX(10);
rectangle.setY(10);
rectangle.setHeight(150);
rectangle.setWidth(150);
rectangle.setFill(Color.web("#FF00FF",0));
```

In contrast to the full transparency of 0, you can set the alpha value to 1 for a fully opaque color:

```
Rectangle rectangle = new Rectangle();

rectangle.setX(10);
rectangle.setY(10);
```

```
rectangle.setHeight(150);
rectangle.setWidth(150);
rectangle.setFill(Color.web("#FF00FF",1));
```

Finally, setting the alpha value to .5 will give you opacity of 50 percent:

```
Rectangle rectangle = new Rectangle();

rectangle.setX(10);
rectangle.setY(10);
rectangle.setHeight(150);
rectangle.setWidth(150);
rectangle.setFill(Color.web("#FF00FF",0.5));

}
```

In the next section, you learn how to create and use gradients. Gradients provide a creative and eye-catching way to fill your shapes.

Using Gradients

You can use two kinds of gradients to fill your shapes: LinearGradients and RadialGradients. LinearGradients are gradients that fill in a straight line from one side of a shape to the opposite side. RadialGradients start the gradient at one point, and the gradient radiates out from that point to fill the shape.

Let's first look at how to apply a LinearGradient to a rectangle.

LinearGradients

The LinearGradient class is contained in the javafx.scene.paint package:

```
import javafx.scene.paint.LinearGradient;
```

You need to learn about seven parameters for the LinearGradient class constructor before you can properly fill a shape with a gradient.

The first four parameters are startX, startY, endX, and endY. These parameters should have a value between 0 and 1. On the x-axis, 0 is the left side of your shape and 1 is the right side of your shape. On the y-axis, 0 is the top of your shape and 1 is the bottom of your shape—if proportional is set to true. Otherwise, the values for the x- and y-coordinates are in the local coordinate system and there will be no gradient stretching. To keep things easy, set proportional to true for now.

Speaking of which, the fifth parameter is the proportional parameter, which accepts a Boolean value and determines how the first four parameters are treated by the class.

The sixth parameter is the CycleMethod, which dictates how the gradient is filled in and repeated. If this value is set to NO_CYCLE, the gradient is filled in using the selected terminal colors. If CycleMethod is set to REFLECT, a mirror effect is used when filling the gradient—from one color to the second and then back again. Finally, if CycleMethod is set to REPEAT, the gradient repeats itself.

The final parameter is the stops parameter, which holds an array of colors that will be used in the gradient. This is a very versatile aspect of JavaFX: Gradients can be made with two or more colors. Each color you add to the gradient is composed of a Color class and an offset attribute. The offset is a number between 0 and 1 that determines where in the gradient the color is placed.

If your head is just about spinning right now, don't feel bad. LinearGradients will make much more sense when you see the code in action. Take a look at the following code.

NOTE
Add the following import statement to your script javafx.scene.paint.Stop.

```
Rectangle rectangle = new Rectangle();
Stop[] gradientStops = new Stop[] {
                    new Stop(0, Color.BLACK),
                    new Stop(1, Color.WHITE)};
LinearGradient lg = new LinearGradient(
                    0,0,1,0,true,CycleMethod.NO_CYCLE,
                    gradientStops);

rectangle.setX(10);
rectangle.setY(10);
rectangle.setHeight(150);
rectangle.setWidth(150);
rectangle.setFill(lg);
```

The preceding code creates the LinearGradient shown in Figure 6-1. This is a fairly standard two-color gradient.

NOTE
If you want the gradient to flow vertically rather than horizontally, flip the third and fourth parameters of LinearGradient.

The stops attribute accepts an array of colors. This means you can add as many colors as you want to the gradient. The following code creates the three-color LinearGradient shown in Figure 6-2:

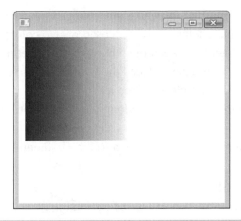

Figure 6-1   A proportionally true, two-color LinearGradient

```
Rectangle rectangle = new Rectangle();
Stop[] gradientStops = new Stop[] {
                      new Stop(0, Color.BLACK),
                      new Stop(0.5, Color.WHITE),
                      new Stop(1, Color.TOMATO)};
LinearGradient lg = new LinearGradient(0,0,1,0,true,
                    CycleMethod.NO_CYCLE,gradientStops);

rectangle.setX(10);
rectangle.setY(10);
rectangle.setHeight(150);
rectangle.setWidth(150);
rectangle.setFill(lg);
```

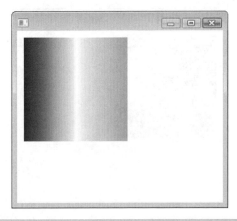

Figure 6-2   A three-color LinearGradient

Notice how the value of the offset attribute changed to accommodate the three-color LinearGradient. When the gradient was composed of two colors, the offsets were 0 and 1. To place a third color exactly between the other two, an offset of .5 needed to be assigned. An offset higher than .5 would have placed the white closer to the right, whereas a value lower than .5 would have put it closer to the left.

By changing the start and end points along the y-axis, you can tilt the gradient as shown in Figure 6-3.

Now let's look at how to create and use a RadialGradient.

RadialGradients

RadialGradients are gradients that, instead of emanating from one side, radiate out from a central point. Whereas LinearGradients work well with rectilinear shapes, RadialGradients work best on circles and ellipses. RadialGradients are in the javafx.scene.paintpackage. You can import this package and the correct class into your code using the following statement:

```
import javafx.scene.paint.RadialGradient;
import javafx.scene.shape.Circle;
```

Because a RadialGradient emanates out from a center point in a circular pattern, you must define a center point and radius. The center point and radius create a circle for the first color of the RadialGradient. The color will then fill the host shape while diffusing into the second color.

The first parameter of the RadialGradient is FocusAngle. The focus angle is the angle of the focal point of the gradient in relationship to the center. Given that the gradient is being mapped around a spheroid, it does not need to correspond directly with the center

Figure 6-3 A three-color skewed LinearGradient

Figure 6-4 A RadialGradient in a circle

of the object it is being mapped to. The FocusAngle is also used with the next parameter, FocusDistance, to determine where the exact focus of the gradient is. The FocusDistance is the distance from the center, along the FocusAngle, to the focus of the gradient.

The RadialGradient class, like the LinearGradient class, also accepts an array of stops to produce gradients of more than two colors. The following code produces the gradient shown in Figure 6-4:

```
Circle circle = new Circle();
Stop[] gradientStops = new Stop[] {
                    new Stop(0, Color.BLACK),
                    new Stop(1, Color.WHITE)};
RadialGradient lg = new RadialGradient(.1,.1,5,5,7,
                true,CycleMethod.NO_CYCLE,gradientStops);

circle.setRadius(70);
circle.setCenterX(100);
circle.setCenterY(100);
circle.setFill(lg);
```

Try This Create a Custom Gradient

Using the skills you learned in Chapter 5, create a new Scene with multiple shapes on it. Once your shapes are in place, use the skills you learned in this chapter to add a different gradient to each one. Change the gradient by mixing different colors on each shape. This is a great way to practice multiple techniques and get instant results.

In this chapter, you learned how to create colors, make gradients, and apply them to shapes. LinearGradients and RadialGradients provide an easy way to add visual interest to your shapes.

In the next chapter, you will learn how to use images in your applications.

Chapter 6 Self Test

1. How many predefined colors are available in the Color class?

2. What are the three methods available in the Color class for mixing colors?

3. True or false? RGB stands for refraction, gradient, and blur.

4. What is the acceptable value range for Hue?

5. In what package is the code for LinearGradients?

6. What is the default value for the proportional parameter?

7. What is the acceptable range of values for startX when proportional is set to true?

8. True or false? The stops parameter tells the gradient what point to stop on.

9. True or false? Gradients can be composed of more than two colors.

10. Which gradient is best for curvilinear shapes?

Chapter 7
Using Images

Key Skills & Concepts

- Using an ImageView

- Loading images

- Loading an image placeholder

Chances are that if you are creating an application with JavaFX, you will need to have some form of interaction with images. Even if your application is not directly related to images or image manipulation, you may need a splash screen, a background, or even an image for use in a control.

This chapter teaches you how to work with images and load them into JavaFX. By the end of this chapter you will be able to add an image file to your project and load it to the screen. The first step in this process is to learn about the ImageView node.

The ImageView Node

Before you can display an image to the screen, you need to add an ImageView node to your scene graph. All images are displayed using the ImageView node. Think of it as the film onto which your pictures are developed. The only purpose for the ImageView node is to display your images using the Image class.

Create a new JavaFX Application project named Chapter7 (as you have done in previous chapters) and remove all of the Hello World code from Chapter7.java.

The class for the ImageView is javafx.scene.image.ImageView.

You must import this package before you can use the ImageView. Instantiate a new ImageView and add it to your Scene, as follows:

```
package Chapter7;

import javafx.application.Application;
import javafx.scene.Scene;
import javafx.scene.image.ImageView;
import javafx.scene.layout.StackPane;
import javafx.stage.Stage;

/**
 *
```

```
 * @author J F DiMarzio
 */
public class Chapter7 extends Application {

    /**
     * @paramargs the command line arguments
     */
    public static void main(String[] args) {
        launch(args);
    }

    @Override
    public void start(Stage primaryStage) {
ImageViewimageView = new ImageView();

StackPane root = new StackPane();
root.getChildren().add(imageView);

primaryStage.setScene(new Scene(root, 300, 250));
primaryStage.show();
    }
}
```

As it is now, the ImageView node will not do anything. Keep in mind that although the ImageView is a node by itself, it really doesn't do much without an image to display. Right now the application will compile and run, but you will be presented with a blank UI; you need to add an image for the ImageView to display. In the next section you use the Image class to help the ImageView display something to the screen.

TIP
The ImageView has attributes that affect the way in which an image is displayed. However, without an image to display, it does not make sense to discuss those attributes now. You will learn about these attributes after sending an image to the ImageView.

The Image Class

The Image class is used to take in image files and format them for display. The Image class and the ImageView node work hand-in-hand to display your images to the screen.

The Image class must be imported before you start working:

```
importjavafx.scene.image.Image;
```

The Image class can read images from various sources. In this section you work with two of these sources: the Web and a local image file. First, let's pull an image from the Internet. The image you will display is http://jfdimarzio.com/butterfly.png. The constructor of the Image class takes a URL for an image to display. The URL of the image—in this case, http://jfdimarzio.com/butterfly.png—is passed to the constructor. This tells the Image class where to look for a valid image to format.

After you have created an Image object, use the setImage() method of the ImageView to set the source of the image you want to write to the scene graph. The width and height properties that govern how the image is displayed are set in the ImageView. You use the setFitWidth() and setFitHeight() methods to tell the ImageView, "I want the image to fit to this width and height," like so:

NOTE
You can use a trick by setting just the width or the height attribute and then using setPreserveRatio() to tell the ImageView to keep the original width/height ratio of the Image—using your one new value.

```
@Override
public void start(Stage primaryStage) {
    Image butterfly = new Image("http://jfdimarzio.com/butterfly.png");
ImageViewimageView = new ImageView();

imageView.setImage(butterfly);
imageView.setFitWidth(300);
imageView.setPreserveRatio(true);

StackPane root = new StackPane();
root.getChildren().add(imageView);

primaryStage.setScene(new Scene(root, 300, 250));
primaryStage.show();
}
```

After you compile and run this code, your application should look like what's shown in Figure 7-1.

JavaFX does a good job of displaying images from a website, and the setup involved in this is fairly straightforward. The url parameter points directly to the image you want to display. However, chances are you are going to want to display images that you package into your application.

If you want to display an image that you have locally, the concept remains the same but the process is slightly different. You will want to think ahead as to how the image will be distributed with the application.

Figure 7-1   Using an image from the Web

You can include an image in the package with your application. That image can then be called from an Image class and displayed using the ImageView. Distributing images in this way is more reliable than displaying them from the Internet. That is, there are more chances for something to go wrong if you are relying on an external website to host your images and you are relying on the Internet connection of that user to access the images.

The first step in displaying a local image is to include that image in your package. Right-click your package and select New | Other. This will open the Create File dialog box. Select the Other category and then select a File Type of Folder. Click the Next button to continue and name your folder. In this case, name the folder **images** and then click Finish. Now you have a folder within your package to keep your images.

TIP
It is always recommended to create a separate folder for your images. This helps you keep your projects standardized and easy to manage.

Next, drag an image from your local drive into the images folder in the NetBeans IDE, as shown in Figure 7-2.

Now that the image is added to your project packages, you can reference it in your code. The key to referencing an image you have added directly to your package is knowing the path to that file.

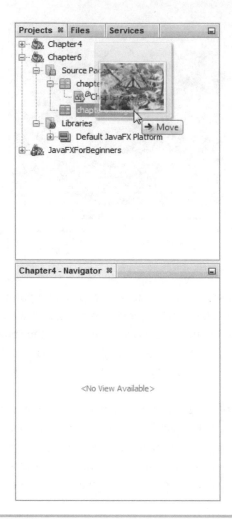

Figure 7-2 Adding an image to your package

You can reference your new image from your images folder by specifying the full path to the image file in the Image constructor. The following code shows an ImageView displaying the butterfly.png file from the images folder:

NOTE
Replace the path in this code with one that points directly to your project and your images folder.

```
@Override
public void start(Stage primaryStage) {
    Image butterfly = new Image(Chapter7Chapter7this.getClass()
                        .getResource("images/butterfly.png")
                        .toExternalForm());
ImageViewimageView = new ImageView(butterfly);


//
imageView.setFitWidth(300);
imageView.setPreserveRatio(true);

StackPane root = new StackPane();
root.getChildren().add(imageView);

primaryStage.setScene(new Scene(root, 300, 250));
primaryStage.show();
}
```

To this point you have learned how to display an image using the Image class and the
ImageView node. Admittedly this is not the most exciting code in the book—it is actually
very basic. However, the real fun can happen once the images are loaded to the Scene.

The following code loads your image, moves it both vertically and horizontally, and
applies a rotation:

```
    Image butterfly - new Image("file:/C:/Users/J F DiMarzio/" +
                        "Documents/NetBeansProjects/Chapter7/" +
                        "src/Chapter7/images/butterfly.png");
ImageViewimageView = new ImageView();

imageView.setImage(butterfly);
imageView.setTranslateX(30);
imageView.setTranslateY(30);
imageView.setRotate(45);
```

The ImageView inherits methods from Node that can be used to set the X and Y
translation of the image. The method setTranslationX() will move the image a number of
points on the X Cartesian coordinate scale relative to the position of the upper-left corner
of the image. Similarly, setTranslateY() and setTranslateZ() will move the image along the
Y and Z Cartesian coordinates, respectively. Finally, the setRotate() method will rotate the
image at its center point a specified number of degrees.

Add the previous code to your .java file so that it looks like this:

```
@Override
public void start(Stage primaryStage) {
    Image butterfly = new Image("file:/C:/Users/J F DiMarzio/" +
```

```
                              "Documents/NetBeansProjects/Chapter7/" +
                              "src/Chapter7/images/butterfly.png");
ImageViewimageView = new ImageView();

imageView.setImage(butterfly);
imageView.setTranslateX(30);
imageView.setTranslateY(30);
imageView.setRotate(45);

imageView.setFitWidth(300);
imageView.setPreserveRatio(true);

StackPane root = new StackPane();
root.getChildren().add(imageView);

primaryStage.setScene(new Scene(root, 300, 250));
primaryStage.show();
}
```

Run this code using your Desktop profile, and you will see the image rotated and moved, as shown in Figure 7-3.

Figure 7-3   Butterfly image rotated and moved

Try This Working with Different Image Types

Take some time before the next chapter to explore how JavaFX displays and works with different images and image types. Using the skills you learned in this chapter, try to display images of different types to JavaFX. Which images files will display? Which image files will not?

For an added level of research, try changing the sizes of the images. Take note of which image types allow you to load up the largest images in the shortest amount of time.

This skill will help you in the future when you need to incorporate images of different types from different developers or sources into one application.

The Canvas

JavaFX provides another API for drawing to the screen. The Canvas API, another subclass of Node, can be used in a scene graph to write to the screen and display shapes, colors, and textures.

The Canvas API uses a GraphicsContext in rendering objects to the screen. The GraphicsContext class fulfills drawing calls from the Canvas API. Just a handful of the available methods for drawing, filling, and writing to the Canvas are used in the example provided in this section.

Let's use the Canvas API to draw two circles to the screen. The first circle is a red filled circle, and the second circle is a black, unfilled outline.

First, set up a new Stage. Instantiate a new Canvas, Group, and GraphicsContext for the new Stage, as follows:

```
public static void main(String[] args) {
        launch(args);
    }

    @Override
    public void start(Stage primaryStage) {
        primaryStage.setTitle("Drawing Operations Test");
        Group root = new Group();
        Canvas canvas = new Canvas(800, 600);
        GraphicsContext gc = canvas.getGraphicsContext2D();
        root.getChildren().add(canvas);
        primaryStage.setScene(new Scene(root, 800, 600));
        primaryStage.show();
    }

    . . .
}
```

With the new Stage and Canvas set, create a new method named drawCircles(). The drawCircles() method will accept a GraphicContext from the Canvas. Then, using the GraphicContext, the drawCircles() method will set up the needed calls to create the two circles in our example:

```
private void drawCircles(GraphicsContext gc) {
    gc.setFill(Color.RED);
    gc.setStroke(Color.BLACK);
    gc.setLineWidth(2);
    gc.fillOval(50, 50, 300, 300);
    gc.strokeOval(50, 50, 300, 300);
}
```

The drawCircles() method uses the GraphicContext to draw two circles on the Canvas. First, setFill() and setStroke() are called to set the corresponding brushes to RED and BLACK, respectively. Then, the width of the brush is set to 2 pixels using the setLineWidth() method. Finally, the circles are drawn using calls to fillOval() and strokeOval().

Compile and run the following code to see two circles drawn on each other, using the GraphicsContext and Canvas API:

```
public class Chapter7 extends Application {

    /**
     * @param args the command line arguments
     */
    public static void main(String[] args) {
        launch(args);
    }

    @Override
    public void start(Stage primaryStage) {
        primaryStage.setTitle("Drawing Operations Test");
        Group root = new Group();
        Canvas canvas = new Canvas(800, 600);
        GraphicsContext gc = canvas.getGraphicsContext2D();
        drawCircles(gc);
        root.getChildren().add(canvas);
        primaryStage.setScene(new Scene(root, 800, 600));
        primaryStage.show();
    }

    private void drawCircles(GraphicsContext gc) {
        gc.setFill(Color.RED);
        gc.setStroke(Color.BLACK);
```

```
        gc.setLineWidth(2);
        gc.fillOval(50, 50, 300, 300);
        gc.strokeOval(50, 50, 300, 300);

    }
}
```

In this chapter you learned to import and display images to your JavaFX Scenes. This is an important skill to have in creating rich environments for your users. However, just displaying images alone will not create an exciting enough environment to stop your users in their tracks.

In Chapter 8 you learn how to apply effects to your images within JavaFX.

Chapter 7 Self Test

1. What node is used to display images?

2. What class is used to write an image to the ImageView node?

3. True or false? An Image class can accept images from the Web.

4. What protocol is used to locate an image in a local directory?

5. True or false? To have an image load in the background, use the BackgroundImage loader.

6. What method allows you to move an image on the x-axis?

7. What class contains the method setRotate(): Image or ImageView?

8. What node is used to display images from an Image class?

9. True or false? The setTranslateY() method moves an image a specified number of inches across the screen.

10. What is the purpose of the setPreserveRatio() method?

Chapter 8
Applying Effects and Transformations

Key Skills & Concepts

- Applying effects to shapes and images
- Moving images in an application
- Rotating images and shapes

In Chapter 7 you learned how to write images to the screen using the Image class and ImageView node. In Chapter 5 you learned how to create different shapes and place them around your application. In this chapter you begin to apply effects and transitions to these images and shapes.

The first section of this chapter covers effects. JavaFX has a comprehensive list of effects you can apply to many objects within your applications. These effects have a stunning impact on your applications and can be used to create almost any desired look or feel.

To begin this chapter, create a new, empty JavaFX Application project (following the instructions covered earlier in the book). Name the project **Chapter8**. You are going to set up Chapter8.java to display the same ImageView and image file you used in Chapter 7. This allows you to experiment with applying effects to an image. You will find that there are several ways to apply effects. For example, effects can be applied to a group of images collectively or to individual images separately. Working with a single image file, you will be applying effects to that image, but the same techniques can be used on multiple images.

Set up your .java file as follows:

```java
package Chapter8;

import javafx.application.Application;
import javafx.scene.Scene;
import javafx.scene.image.Image;
import javafx.scene.image.ImageView;
import javafx.scene.layout.StackPane;
import javafx.stage.Stage;

/**
 *
 * @author J F DiMarzio
 */
public class Chapter8 extends Application {

    /**
```

```
 * @param args the command line arguments
 */
public static void main(String[] args) {
    launch(args);
}

@Override
public void start(Stage primaryStage) {
    Image image = new Image("http://jfdimarzio.com/butterfly.png");
    ImageView imageView = new ImageView();

    imageView.setImage(image);
    applyEffects(imageView);

    StackPane root = new StackPane();
    root.getChildren().add(imageView);
    primaryStage.setScene(new Scene(root, 800, 600));
    primaryStage.show();
}

private void applyEffects(ImageView imageView)
{

}
}
```

The major difference between this code and what you have used in the previous chapters is the inclusion of a method called applyEffects(), which is where you put all the code for your effects. This method will apply a specific effect to your ImageView using code you will add soon.

```
private void applyEffects(ImageView imageView)
    {

    }
```

This method takes your ImageView as a parameter. You will be writing code that applies an effect to the ImageView that is passed into applyEffects(). The method will then return to the main body of the code, and your image will be rendered with the effect applied.

NOTE
This design, where a common method is used to apply a specific effect to an image, may not be practical in a real working application. However, it lends itself very nicely to learning how effects work by separating the code.

Figure 8-1 The image before effects are applied

When compiled, this JavaFX app, as it is, should produce an image like the one in Figure 8-1.

This .java file, in its current state, will be the base you use for the rest of this chapter. All the effects and transformations you learn about in this chapter are demonstrated using this application. The first section of this chapter covers effects, which is followed by a discussion of transformations.

Effects

JavaFX is capable of rendering stunning and complex effects. Images and effects can be blended, blurred, and shadowed. Such effects can be very compelling and can be used to create applications that engage your users.

These effects can be applied to almost any node in JavaFX. All the standard effects available to you in JavaFX are in the javafx.scene.effect package. Import this package to begin working with JavaFX effects if you have not done so already:

```
import javafx.scene.effect.*;
```

TIP

To this point, you have explicitly stated which items in each package you want to import. However, the **.*** notation tells JavaFX to import all the items within a particular package. Therefore, the statement **import javafx.scene.effect.*** will give you access to all the effects in the effect package.

The first effect you will use is Bloom.

Bloom

The Bloom effect takes the areas of higher contrast in your image and makes them appear to glow by overrunning these areas of high contract and bleeding them into the surrounding image. The amount of Bloom applied to the node is controlled by the threshold parameter, which accepts a value between 0 and 1, with 0 being no effect at all.

Use the applyEffects() method in the Chapter8.java file to apply the Bloom effect to the butterfly.png image. Every ImageView node has an effect parameter. This parameter is set to the effect you want to apply to that ImageView.

TIP

You are working with an ImageView in this chapter because you just worked with it in Chapter 7. However, ImageViews are not the only nodes you can apply effects to. Every node contains an effect parameter that you can apply an effect to.

You can now edit the applyEffects() method to apply the Bloom effect to the butterfly image. Add the following lines to the applyEffects() method:

```
Bloom bloom = new Bloom();
bloom.setThreshold(.5);
imageView.setEffect(bloom);
```

This sets the effect property of the ImageView to the Bloom effect. The threshold is set to .5 to give you a good idea of what the Bloom effect can do. You can adjust the threshold to your liking to achieve the desired effect. Your applyEffects() method should now look like this:

```
private void applyEffects(ImageView imageView)
{
    Bloom bloom = new Bloom();
```

```
        bloom.setThreshold(.5);
        imageView.setEffect(bloom);
}
```

The entire finished application is shown here:

```
package Chapter8;

import javafx.application.Application;
import javafx.scene.Scene;
import javafx.scene.effect.Bloom;
import javafx.scene.image.Image;
import javafx.scene.image.ImageView;
import javafx.scene.layout.StackPane;
import javafx.stage.Stage;

/**
 *
 * @author J F DiMarzio
 */
public class Chapter8 extends Application {

    /**
     * @param args the command line arguments
     */
    public static void main(String[] args) {
        launch(args);
    }

    @Override
    public void start(Stage primaryStage) {
        Image image = new Image("http://jfdimarzio.com/butterfly.png");
        ImageView imageView = new ImageView();

        imageView.setImage(image);
        applyEffects(imageView);

        StackPane root = new StackPane();
        root.getChildren().add(imageView);
        primaryStage.setScene(new Scene(root, 800, 600));
        primaryStage.show();
    }

    private void applyEffects(ImageView imageView)
    {
        Bloom bloom = new Bloom();
        bloom.setThreshold(.5);
        imageView.setEffect(bloom);
    }
}
```

Figure 8-2   Butterfly with the Bloom effect

Compile your JavaFX app and run it to produce an image with the Bloom effect applied, as shown in Figure 8-2.

Next, you learn about the ColorAdjust effect.

ColorAdjust

As the name suggests, the ColorAdjust effect allows you to adjust the color of your node. In much the same way that you adjust the picture on your television, JavaFX lets you adjust your images. ColorAdjust contains parameters that allow you to adjust the contrast, brightness, hue, and saturation.

All the parameters for the ColorAdjust effect, with the exception of input, accept a double value. You can assign a value between –1.0 and 1.0 to each of the following: contrast, brightness, hue, and saturation. However, you do not necessarily need to assign a value to all the parameters. For instance, if you just want to adjust the contrast of an image, you only have to specify a value for the contrast parameter, and JavaFX will automatically assign a 0 to the others. (Note that JavaFX will not auto-assign a 0 to contrast because it has a default value of 1.)

For this example, you will assign .5 to each parameter and then assign the effect to the butterfly. Add the following code to the applyEffects() method:

```
ColorAdjust colorAdjust = new ColorAdjust();
colorAdjust.setBrightness(.5);
colorAdjust.setContrast(.5);
colorAdjust.setHue(.5);
colorAdjust.setSaturation(.5);
```

In previous chapters, you used the LineBuilder and the RectangleBuilder. In this example, you can use the ColorAdjustBuilder to really clean up this code and make your life a little easier.

```
colorAdjustBuilder.create().brightness(.5)
                           .contrast(.5).hue(.5)
                           .saturation(.5).build();
```

The structure of the ColorAdjust effect should look familiar if you followed along with the previous example. Effects, as a whole, are not very complicated to apply once you have done it a couple times. Your complete applyEffects() method should look like this:

```
private void applyEffects(ImageView imageView)
{
    ColorAdjust colorAdjust = new
ColorAdjustBuilder.create().brightness(.5).contrast(.5)
                           .hue(.5).saturation(.5).build();
;

    imageView.setEffect(colorAdjust);
}
```

Compile your app and run it. You will see an image like the one shown in Figure 8-3.

Notice that the butterfly colors have been adjusted and appear almost animated. Experiment with assigning different values to each parameter.

The next effect you learn about is GaussianBlur.

GaussianBlur

GaussianBlur provides a very smooth blurring effect to a node. Behind the scenes, the effect works on something called the *Gaussian algorithm.* This algorithm works in a circular pattern from each pixel to smooth the appearance. Because this algorithm works in a circular pattern, the parameter you need to work with is the radius parameter, which controls how far out from each pixel the Gaussian algorithm is applied.

Figure 8-3   Butterfly modified using ColorAdjust

You can specify a value from 0 to 63 for the radius of the GaussianBlur. A value of 0 would be little to no blur in the original image, whereas a value of 63 would be an extreme blur. The following code implements a GaussianBlur with a radius of 10 (which is the default):

```
GaussianBlur blur = new GaussianBlur();
blur.setRadius(10);
```

Apply the GaussianBlur to your applyEffects() function as follows:

```
private void applyEffects(ImageView imageView)
{
    GaussianBlur blur = new GaussianBlur();

    imageView.setEffect(blur);
}
```

Run your completed app, which blurs the background with a radius of 10. The result is shown in Figure 8-4.

Notice that the butterfly is slightly blurred, but still recognizable. Now change the radius to 60 and recompile the app. The results are shown in Figure 8-5.

GaussianBlur is particularly effective when you are trying to resize images. Occasionally an image can become distorted when it is resized, especially if the image is quite sharp before it is resized. Applying a very light GaussianBlur before resizing the image (in systems that do not do so automatically) can make the resized image less distorted.

You learn about the Glow effect next.

Figure 8-4   Butterfly with a GaussianBlur radius of 10

Figure 8-5 Butterfly with a GaussianBlur radius of 60

Glow

The Glow effect, as the name suggests, makes your node appear to glow. The amount of glow applied to the node is controlled by the level parameter. The level of glow you can apply to a node ranges from 0 to 1. Assigning no level for the Glow effect will cause JavaFX to use a default of .3.

Earlier in this chapter you learned about the Bloom effect, which applied a Glow-like effect to your node. The difference between Bloom and Glow is in the way the glow is applied. Whereas Bloom only applies a glow to the higher contrast parts of an image, Glow works on the entire image.

The following code shows your applyEffects() method with a Glow level of .5:

```
Glow glow = new Glow();
glow.setLevel(.5);
```

Replace the applyEffects() method in your current .java file with this one. Your full .java file should now look like this:

```java
package Chapter8;

import javafx.application.Application;
import javafx.scene.Scene;
import javafx.scene.effect.Glow;
import javafx.scene.image.Image;
import javafx.scene.image.ImageView;
import javafx.scene.layout.StackPane;
import javafx.stage.Stage;

/**
 *
 * @author J F DiMarzio
 */
public class Chapter8 extends Application {

    /**
     * @param args the command line arguments
     */
    public static void main(String[] args) {
        launch(args);
    }

    @Override
    public void start(Stage primaryStage) {
        Image image = new Image("http://jfdimarzio.com/butterfly.png");
        ImageView imageView = new ImageView();

        imageView.setImage(image);
        applyEffects(imageView);

        StackPane root = new StackPane();
        root.getChildren().add(imageView);
        primaryStage.setScene(new Scene(root, 800, 600));
        primaryStage.show();
    }

    private void applyEffects(ImageView imageView)
    {
        Glow glow = new Glow();
        glow.setLevel(.5);
        imageView.setEffect(glow);
    }
}
```

Compile and run your app. Your butterfly image should glow like the one shown in Figure 8-6.

The next effect you learn about is the DropShadow effect.

Figure 8-6 Butterfly with a Glow of .5

DropShadow

The DropShadow effect creates a shadow under your node by replicating the node in a shadow color and offsetting the "shadow" image by a specific amount under your source node. Quite a few parameters are needed to configure DropShadow:

- **radius** Used like the radius parameter for GaussianBlur.
- **height/width** Can be used instead of radius, and has the same effect.
- **spread** The opacity of the shadow. A value of 0 creates a very light, scattered shadow, whereas a value of 1 produces a dark, sharp shadow.
- **blurType** The algorithm used to create the shadow. This can be set to Gaussian, ONE_PASS_BOX, TWO_PASS_BOX, or THREE_PASS_BOX. These blur types

use a box blur algorithm to smooth the image. You can specify whether you want the algorithm to be applied in one, two, or three different passes. The image blur gets progressively smoother with each pass. Therefore, a blur that has been set with THREE_PASS_BOX will be much smoother looking than a blur that has ONE_PASS_BOX.

● **color** The color of the shadow defaults to BLACK.

Modify your applyEffects() method to create a DropShadow effect, as follows:

```
private void applyEffects(ImageView imageView)
{
    DropShadow dropShadow = new DropShadow();
    dropShadow.setBlurType(BlurType.THREE_PASS_BOX);

    dropShadow.setOffsetX(10);
    dropShadow.setOffsetY(10);
    dropShadow.setRadius(10);
    dropShadow.setSpread(.2);
    imageView.setEffect(dropShadow);
}
```

Take a good look at the code that follows. One change had to be made just for this effect. The size of the scene has been adjusted from 800×600 to 850×650 just to let you see the DropShadow effect. (You can change it back for the next effect.)

```
package Chapter8;

import javafx.application.Application;
import javafx.scene.Scene;
import javafx.scene.effect.DropShadow;
import javafx.scene.image.Image;
import javafx.scene.image.ImageView;
import javafx.scene.layout.StackPane;
import javafx.scene.paint.Color;
import javafx.stage.Stage;

/**
 *
 * @author J F DiMarzio
 */
public class Chapter8 extends Application {

    /**
     * @param args the command line arguments
     */
```

```
public static void main(String[] args) {
    launch(args);
}

@Override
public void start(Stage primaryStage) {
    Image image = new Image("http://jfdimarzio.com/butterfly.png");
    ImageView imageView = new ImageView();

    imageView.setImage(image);
    applyEffects(imageView);

    StackPane root = new StackPane();
    root.getChildren().add(imageView);
    primaryStage.setScene(new Scene(root, 850, 650));
    primaryStage.show();
}

private void applyEffects(ImageView imageView)
{
    DropShadow dropShadow = new DropShadow();
    dropShadow.setBlurType(BlurType.THREE_PASS_BOX);
    dropShadow.setColor(Color.BLACK);
    dropShadow.setOffsetX(10);
    dropShadow.setOffsetY(10);
    dropShadow.setRadius(10);
    dropShadow.setSpread(.2);
    imageView.setEffect(dropShadow);
}
}
```

This script produces a shadow under the butterfly like the one shown in Figure 8-7.

The DropShadow effect works by creating a blurred copy of your original image. The copy is placed under the original image and then offset so you can see it. You can use the Shadow effect if you want to control this process yourself.

The Shadow effect creates a blurred, colored image based on your original. However, it does not re-add an unaltered copy of your image to the scene. You are literally just left with the shadow of your image. You will have to manually add another instance of your image to the scene to complete the effect.

Using the Shadow effect over the DropShadow effect has its advantages, though. For example, it can come in quite handy if you want to project the shadow onto a location detached from the original image.

You learn about the Lighting effect next.

Figure 8-7 Butterfly with DropShadow

Lighting

The Lighting effect is by far the most complex effect offered in JavaFX. Lighting can be used to add a dimension of realism to an otherwise flat object. Although Lighting is a complex effect to set up, it is very rewarding if used correctly.

The main parameter of the Lighting effect is Light, which represents the type of light from the javafx.scene.effect.light package. Three different classes can be used for Light:

- Distant
- Point
- Spot

NOTE

The relationship between Lighting and Light is that Lighting defines how Light is used by the effect.

Each of these Light types has its own set of parameters that controls the specific type of light.

Distant

The Distant class takes three parameters that configure and control the light: azimuth, elevation, and color.

```
Light.Distant distant = new Light.Distant();
distant.setAzimuth(45);
distant.setElevation(45);
distant.setColor(Color.RED);
```

The azimuth is the angle at which the light is shining onto your object, whereas the elevation is the height (can also be negative) of the light source.

Update your applyEffects() method to implement the Lighting effect using Distant. Set the azimuth of the light to 45, the elevation to 45, and the color to RED, as shown next. Do not forget to import the javafx.scene.paint.Color.* package to manipulate the color of the light.

```
private void applyEffects(ImageView imageView)
{
    Lighting lighting = new Lighting();
    lighting.setLight(new Light.Distant(45,45,Color.RED));

    imageView.setEffect(lighting);
}
```

Compile your app and run it to apply a red-colored distant lighting effect to the butterfly. The result is shown in Figure 8-8.

PointLight

The Point light class takes four parameters, as follows:

```
Light.Point point = new Light.Point();
point.setX();
point.setY();
point.setZ();
point.setColor();
```

Figure 8-8 Butterfly with red Distant light applied

The x-, y-, and z-coordinates that you provide here indicate the position of the light in 3D space. Just as you did with Distant, edit your applyEffects() method to use a Point at position x150, y50, z50, as shown here:

```
private void applyEffects(ImageView imageView)
{
    Lighting lighting = new Lighting();
    lighting.setLight(new Light.Point(150,50,50, Color.YELLOW));

    imageView.setEffect(lighting);
}
```

Your image should look like Figure 8-9 after you compile and run your app.

Figure 8-9   Butterfly with a yellow Point light

Spot

Spot takes the same parameters as Point, with the addition of the SpecularExponent. The SpecularExponent controls the focus of the light's beam, much like some flashlights. However, Spot also adds a few other properties to guide where the light is pointing. These new properties are pointsAtX, pointsAtY, and pointsAtZ.

The following applyEffects() method will apply a Spot lighting effect to the butterfly. Notice that the three properties that have been added are not part of the constructor.

```
private void applyEffects(ImageView imageView)
{
    Lighting lighting = new Lighting();
    Light.Spot spot = new Light.Spot(150,50,50,1,Color.WHITE);
    spot.setPointsAtX(400);
    spot.setPointsAtY(400);
```

```
        spot.setPointsAtZ(-10);
        lighting.setLight(spot);

        imageView.setEffect(lighting);
}
```

Compile your app; the image will look like the one shown in Figure 8-10.
Next, you learn about the SepiaTone effect.

SepiaTone

The SepiaTone effect is designed to emulate the look of older Daguerreotype film. Early film was tinted with Sepia to add color to the prints. This process can be emulated with the SepiaTone effect, which takes a level parameter to adjust the amount of effect applied to the node. The level can be a value between 0 and 1.

Figure 8-10   Butterfly with Spot lighting

Take a look at the following full .java code:

```java
package Chapter8;

import javafx.application.Application;
import javafx.scene.Scene;
import javafx.scene.effect.SepiaTone;
import javafx.scene.image.Image;
import javafx.scene.image.ImageView;
import javafx.scene.layout.StackPane;
import javafx.stage.Stage;

/**
 *
 * @author J F DiMarzio
 */
public class Chapter8 extends Application {

    /**
     * @param args the command line arguments
     */
    public static void main(String[] args) {
        launch(args);
    }

    @Override
    public void start(Stage primaryStage) {
        Image image = new Image("http://jfdimarzio.com/butterfly.png");
        ImageView imageView = new ImageView();

        imageView.setImage(image);
        applyEffects(imageView);

        StackPane root = new StackPane();
        root.getChildren().add(imageView);
        primaryStage.setScene(new Scene(root, 800, 600));
        primaryStage.show();
    }

    private void applyEffects(ImageView imageView)
    {
        SepiaTone sepia = new SepiaTone();
        sepia.setLevel(1);

        imageView.setEffect(sepia);
    }
}
```

Figure 8-11 shows the results of this code.

In the next section of this chapter, you learn about transformations and how they differ from effects.

Figure 8-11 SepiaTone applied to the butterfly image

Transformations

A transformation does not change the node the way an effect does. Transformations are affine (meaning all straight lines are preserved) and can be applied to all nodes in a scene graph. Simple transformations can be used for translations, rotation, scaling, or shearing along an axis.

The three different kinds of transformations are xy transformations, rotations, and transformations of perspective. (Strictly speaking, the perspective transform is actually an effect and is non-affine; however, it is covered here as a transformation along the z-axis.) These transformation types are detailed next.

XY Transformations

In this chapter you have been working with a script that contains two ImageView nodes: background and butterfly. Take a look at the following code. In this code, you move the butterfly ImageView –50 pixels along the x-axis and –50 pixels along the y-axis using translation transformations:

```
public void start(Stage primaryStage) {
    Image image = new Image("http://jfdimarzio.com/butterfly.png");
    ImageView imageView = new ImageView();

    imageView.setImage(image);
    applyEffects(imageView);
    imageView.setTranslateX(-50);
    imageView.setTranslateY(-50);

    StackPane root = new StackPane();
    root.getChildren().add(imageView);
    primaryStage.setScene(new Scene(root, 800, 600));
    primaryStage.show();
}
```

The ImageView node has properties named translateX and translateY. These properties are used to move the ImageView around the Scene. Figure 8-12 shows this translation.

Rotation

Rotating an ImageView is just as easy as moving it along an axis. The ImageView node has a property named rotate. Simply set the rotate property of the ImageView to the number of degrees you want to rotate the image. For example, take a look at the following code, which rotates the butterfly image 45 degrees. The result is shown in Figure 8-13.

```
public void start(Stage primaryStage) {
    Image image = new Image("http://jfdimarzio.com/butterfly.png");
    ImageView imageView = new ImageView();

    imageView.setImage(image);
    applyEffects(imageView);
imageView.setRotate(45);

    StackPane root = new StackPane();
    root.getChildren().add(imageView);
    primaryStage.setScene(new Scene(root, 800, 600));
    primaryStage.show();
}
```

Figure 8-12 The Butterfly image translated

Next, you learn about PerspectiveTransform—a member of the Effects package that transforms the perspective of your node.

PerspectiveTransform

PerspectiveTransform alters the perspective of a node. The transform is a non-affine transform that maps an arbitrary quadrilateral into another arbitrary quadrilateral while preserving the straightness of lines. Unlike an affine transformation, the parallelism of lines in the source is not necessarily preserved in the output. This is achieved by giving you control over the x- and y-coordinates of each corner of the node.

Figure 8-13 Butterfly rotated 45 degrees

PerspectiveTransform takes eight parameters for the x- and y-axes of the upper-left, upper-right, lower-left, and lower-right corners. Take a look at the following code for the applyEffects() method:

```
private void applyEffects(ImageView imageView)
{
    PerspectiveTransform transform = new PerspectiveTransform();
    transform.setLlx(100);
    transform.setLly(350);
    transform.setLrx(400);
    transform.setLry(550);
    transform.setUlx(100);
    transform.setUly(100);
```

```
        transform.setUrx(400);
        transform.setUry(100);
    imageView.setEffect(transform);
}
```

In this example, all the coordinates for each corner have been set. It takes a little practice to get the desired effect when using the PerspectiveTransform, so you will want to experiment with the different coordinates. The preceding code produces the result shown in Figure 8-14.

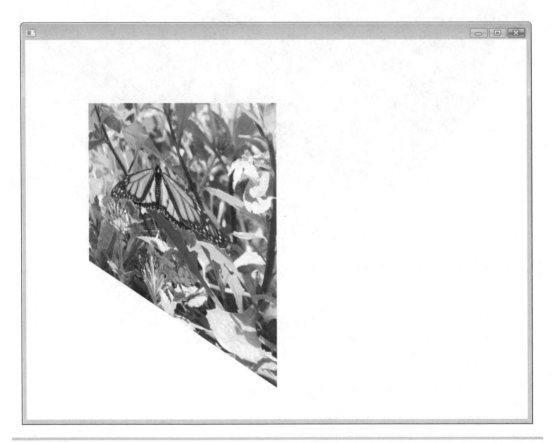

Figure 8-14   Butterfly with PerspectiveTransform

Try This Combining Multiple Effects

The saying "You can't have too much of a good thing" is especially true of JavaFX effects. It is rare when working with an image that you will have to apply just one effect. Often, you will need to apply multiple effects to an image to get the desired look.

Using the skills you acquired in this chapter, create a new project with an image in it. Apply multiple effects to the image at the same time and adjust the properties of these effects to create new and exciting images.

This concludes the chapter on effects and transformations. In the next chapter you will begin to tackle some basic animation.

Chapter 8 Self Test

1. What package needs to be included to work with effects in JavaFX?

2. What effect adjusts only the higher contrast areas of your node to make them glow?

3. True or false? All the parameters of ColorAdjust default to 0 if they are not specified.

4. What parameter needs to be specified to create a GaussianBlur effect?

5. What is the difference between Glow and Bloom?

6. True or false? You do not need to specify both a radius and a height/width for a DropShadow effect.

7. Which effect takes all the opaque areas of your image and makes them transparent?

8. What are the three different lights that can be used in the Lighting effect?

9. What does the following code do?

   ```
   imageView.setRotate(45);
   ```

10. How many parameters need to be set to create a PerspectiveTransform effect?

Chapter 9
Basic Animation

Key Skills & Concepts

- Using Timelines
- Creating paths
- Using KeyFrames and KeyValues

This chapter introduces you to the world of basic JavaFX animation. Whether you want to create animated text and fly-ins or gain knowledge for creating games, basic animation is the place to begin.

You will need to master three basic topics when tackling basic JavaFX animation:

- Timelines
- KeyFrames and KeyValues
- Paths

To begin this chapter, open NetBeans and create a new, empty JavaFX application named **Chapter9**. Based on previous chapters, after you remove the Hello World code, the contents of the Chapter9.java file should look as follows:

```
package Chapter9;

import javafx.application.Application;
import javafx.scene.Scene;
import javafx.scene.layout.StackPane;
import javafx.stage.Stage;

/**
 *
 * @author J F DiMarzio
 */
public class Chapter9 extends Application {

    /**
     * @param args the command line arguments
     */
    public static void main(String[] args) {
        launch(args);
    }
```

```
    @Override
    public void start(Stage primaryStage) {

        StackPane root = new StackPane();
        primaryStage.setScene(new Scene(root, 600, 480));
        primaryStage.show();
    }
}
```

The first section of this chapter covers Timelines.

Timelines

All animation, whether it is "traditional" hand-drawn animation or computer-based animation, is controlled by timing. What actions occur and when, the length of time it takes to walk from one side of a room to another, and syncing the dialogue to a character's mouth movements are all actions that are controlled by some sense of timing. The timing of the animation dictates when each action begins, when it ends, and how long it lasts.

In JavaFX, animation can be moving objects around on the screen, but it can also be something like a highlight being applied to a button on a mouse over or the expansion of a pane in an menu.

Timing is critical to smooth animation. If there is too much time between each frame of animation, it will look slow and jerky to the user. If there is too little time between each frame, the animation will be too fast. This is why timing is so critical.

In JavaFX, the timing of animation is controlled by a Timeline. A Timeline takes a set of KeyFrames and KeyValues to modify properties of your application over time. The class that defines JavaFX Timelines is javafx.animation.Timeline.

The purpose of a Timeline is to break down frames of animation into "stops," by time. This means that if you tell a Timeline where you want an object to be one second from now, and then five seconds from now, the Timeline will modify a value that you can apply to your object. The Timeline takes on the responsibility of producing a smooth increment of values that can be used to represent the movement of your object over the time you specify in your keyframes. This may sound a bit confusing now, but it will make a lot more sense when you see a Timeline in action.

A Timeline is broken down into a collection of keyframes. A *keyframe* is a point at which you want one or more KeyValues to be set to defined values. The Timeline then interpolates between the defined values automatically. For example, you are going to make an animation of a ball moving from the top of the screen to the bottom. Therefore, your keyframes will represent the start of your animation at the top of the screen as well as the end of your animation at bottom of the screen, as shown in Figures 9-1 and 9-2, respectively. The job of the Timeline is to fill in the space in between.

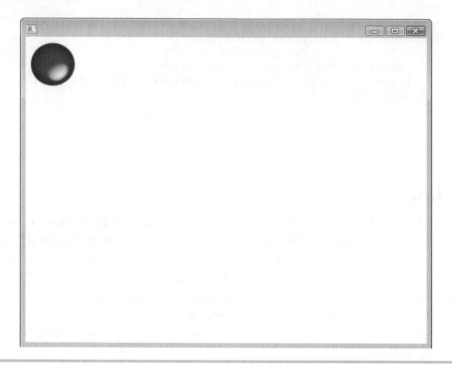

Figure 9-1 The first ball keyframe

You are now going to animate a ball image used from http://jfdimarzio.com/ball.png. You will make the ball image move down the scene, along the y-axis. To begin, you need to create a group.

Why a group? A group is a collection of nodes. In this case you are going to need a group to hold your ImageView and the ball image. The StackPane that you have been using in the previous chapters allows you to stack nodes, but it doesn't allow them to be freely moved around the scene. To animate an image, you need to literally manipulate the x-, y-, or z-coordinate of the image. A StackPane simply doesn't allow that natively.

To get around this issue, you are going to create a group that can be freely moved around the scene. You will then add the image to the group.

The following code sets up your group and image calls:

```
package Chapter9;

import javafx.application.Application;
import javafx.scene.Group;
import javafx.scene.Scene;
```

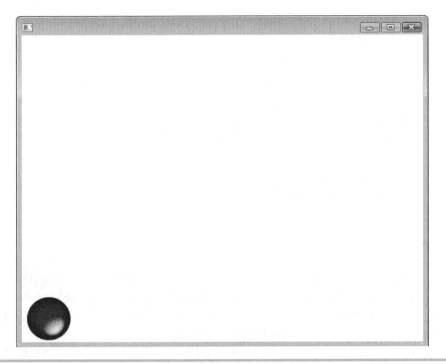

Figure 9-2 The second ball keyframe

```
import javafx.scene.image.Image;
import javafx.scene.image.ImageView;
import javafx.stage.Stage;

/**
 *
 * @author J F DiMarzio
 */
public class Chapter9 extends Application {

    /**
     * @param args the command line arguments
     */
    public static void main(String[] args) {
        launch(args);
    }

    @Override
    public void start(Stage primaryStage) {
        ImageView imageView = new ImageView();
```

```
        Image ball = new Image("http://jfdimarzio.com/ball.png");
        imageView.setImage(ball);

        primaryStage.setHeight(480);
        primaryStage.setWidth(600);

        Group group = new Group();
        Scene scene = new Scene(group);
        group.getChildren().add(imageView);


        primaryStage.setScene(scene);
        primaryStage.show();


    }
}
```

If you have read Chapters 7 and 8, you will recognize most of this code. Therefore, this is a quick overview. The first section contains the image and ImageView. Next, you set the size of the Stage and create new Group and Scene nodes. The Group is added to the Scene's constructor, and the ImageView is added to the Group.

Once your image, group, and scene are created, you can begin to set up your Timeline.

To use the Timeline, you will need to add one or more KeyFrames to it. Each KeyFrame has one or more KeyValues. The KeyValue specifies what property of the ImageView (or any node) you want to modify, and the value you want to modify it to. In this example, you are going to modify the y-translation property of the image to 370. When the app starts, the image will be translated by zero pixels on the y-axis; the Timeline will use the KeyFrame and its KeyValue to interpolate the y-translation between 0 and 370.

Now you can create a KeyFrame that takes your KeyValue and applies a specific amount of time to it. For this example, you position the KeyFrame 2 seconds after the Timeline starts. Finally, add the KeyFrame to the Timeline. The Timeline will do the rest for you. Here is the code:

```
package Chapter9;

import javafx.animation.KeyFrame;
import javafx.animation.KeyValue;
import javafx.animation.Timeline;
import javafx.application.Application;
import javafx.scene.Group;
import javafx.scene.Scene;
import javafx.scene.image.Image;
```

```
import javafx.scene.image.ImageView;
import javafx.stage.Stage;
import javafx.util.Duration;

/**
 *
 * @author J F DiMarzio
 */
public class Chapter9 extends Application {

    /**
     * @param args the command line arguments
     */
    public static void main(String[] args) {
        launch(args);
    }

    @Override
    public void start(Stage primaryStage) {
        ImageView imageView = new ImageView();
        Image ball = new Image("http://jfdimarzio.com/ball.png");
        imageView.setImage(ball);

        primaryStage.setHeight(480);
        primaryStage.setWidth(600);

        Group group = new Group();
        Scene scene = new Scene(group);
        group.getChildren().add(imageView);

        primaryStage.setScene(scene);
        primaryStage.show();

        Timeline timeLine = new Timeline();

        KeyValue keyValue = new KeyValue(imageView.translateYProperty(),370);
        KeyFrame frame = new KeyFrame(Duration.seconds(2),keyValue);
        timeLine.getKeyFrames().add(frame);
        timeLine.play();
    }
}
```

Run this app and you will see the ball image move from the top of the screen to the bottom.

This process is good for simple motions, but what if you want to move your ball in a more elaborate way? The next section of this chapter covers animating your images along a path.

Animating Along a Path

If you want to do a lot of math—and some tricky calculations—you can create a lot of movements with the animation style explained in the previous section. However, if you really want to do some complex animation, such as moving an object around the screen in a curving motion, you will want to use path animation, which is another method that JavaFX has for creating animation that allows you to move an object around a predefined path. In this section you learn how to create a path using knowledge you picked up in previous chapters. You then use this path to animate the ball.

The concept here is that you can create a path using lines, arcs, and points. JavaFX will then animate your image moving along this path.

To begin, set up your Chapter9.java file as shown here:

```
package Chapter9;

import javafx.application.Application;
import javafx.scene.Group;
import javafx.scene.Scene;
import javafx.scene.image.Image;
import javafx.scene.image.ImageView;
import javafx.stage.Stage;

/**
 *
 * @author J F DiMarzio
 */
public class Chapter9 extends Application {

    /**
     * @param args the command line arguments
     */
    public static void main(String[] args) {
        launch(args);
    }

    @Override
    public void start(Stage primaryStage) {
        ImageView imageView = new ImageView();
        Image ball = new Image("http://jfdimarzio.com/ball.png");
        imageView.setImage(ball);

        primaryStage.setHeight(480);
        primaryStage.setWidth(600);

        Group group = new Group();
```

```
        Scene scene = new Scene(group);
        group.getChildren().add(imageView);

        primaryStage.setScene(scene);
        primaryStage.show();
    }
}
```

Similar to what you have seen before, this code grabs the same ball image you have been working with and creates a group. In the previous section, you added a Timeline to this code to animate the ball image travelling up and down the y-axis. For this example, you are going to animate the ball moving around an abstract path.

The next step is to create the path you want your ball image to travel along. You will use a Path node to create this path. The node accepts a collection of elements to create a path from. You can easily create a group of elements that makes an abstractly shaped path. The following piece of code defines a small element array with some basic line-based shapes:

```
...
Path path = new Path();
ArcTo arc1 = new ArcTo();
ArcTo arc2 = new ArcTo();

arc1.setX(350);
arc1.setY(350);
arc1.setRadiusX(150);
arc1.setRadiusY(300);

arc2.setX(150);
arc2.setY(150);
arc2.setRadiusX(150);
arc2.setRadiusY(300);


path.getElements().addAll(new MoveTo(150f, 150f), arc1, arc2);
...
```

There is nothing too complex or tricky about what is happening here. You have created a collection of elements and added them to a Path. The elements contained within the Path are MoveTo and two instances of ArcTo. The combination of these elements creates a path your ball can follow.

The MoveTo element does exactly what the name suggests: It moves you to a specific point on the Cartesian grid. In this case, it moves you to x150, y150. You are specifying this as your first element to cleanly move the starting point of your path before you start "drawing."

The next two elements draw arcs. The first ArcTo element draws an arc from the last position of the point (in this case, x150, y150, thanks to the MoveTo element). The second ArcTo draws another arc from the end point of the last arc.

The JavaFX animation package can now take this Path node and use it to animate your ball using a PathTransition:

```
PathTransition pathTransition = PathTransitionBuilder().create();

pathTransition.duration(Duration.seconds(5))

pathTransition.node(group)
pathTransition.path(path) pathTransition.orientation(OrientationType.
ORTHOGONAL_TO_TANGENT)
pathTransition.build();

pathTransition.play();
```

To create your animation, you use a PathTransition class, which takes in a few familiar parameters. Like Timeline, PathTransition can accept parameters for AutoReverse, CycleCount, and an interpolator—if you choose to use them. However, it is the node, path, duration, and orientation that you want to focus on for this animation.

The node is the object you want animated. In this case, the ball image from the image group. The ball is assigned to the node in the PathTransition class. The node will be animated along the path you created earlier. Use the setPath() method of the PathTransition to add.

Finally, the orientation parameter specifies the position of the node as it is animated along the path. If you do not specify an orientation, the image will remain in whatever orientation it is in when it is drawn to the screen. Setting the orientation to ORTHOGONAL_TO_ TANGENT tells JavaFX to change the orientation of the node as it moves along the path. This change in orientation gives the animation a more organic feel.

The full path animation code should look as follows:

```
package Chapter9;

import javafx.animation.PathTransition;
import javafx.animation.PathTransition.OrientationType;
import javafx.application.Application;
import javafx.scene.Group;
import javafx.scene.Scene;
import javafx.scene.image.Image;
import javafx.scene.image.ImageView;
import javafx.scene.shape.ArcTo;
import javafx.scene.shape.MoveTo;
import javafx.scene.shape.Path;
import javafx.stage.Stage;
import javafx.util.Duration;
```

```
/**
 *
 * @author J F DiMarzio
 */
public class Chapter9 extends Application {

    /**
     * @param args the command line arguments
     */
    public static void main(String[] args) {
        launch(args);
    }

    @Override
    public void start(Stage primaryStage) {
        ImageView imageView = new ImageView();
        Image ball = new Image("http://jfdimarzio.com/ball.png");
        imageView.setImage(ball);

        primaryStage.setHeight(480);
        primaryStage.setWidth(600);

        Group group = new Group();
        Scene scene = new Scene(group);
        group.getChildren().add(imageView);

        primaryStage.setScene(scene);
        primaryStage.show();

        Path path = new Path();
        ArcTo arc1 = new ArcTo();
        ArcTo arc2 = new ArcTo();

        arc1.setX(350);
        arc1.setY(350);
        arc1.setRadiusX(150);
        arc1.setRadiusY(300);

        arc2.setX(150);
        arc2.setY(150);
        arc2.setRadiusX(150);
        arc2.setRadiusY(300);

        path.getElements().add (new MoveTo (150f, 150f));
        path.getElements().add (arc1);
        path.getElements().add (arc2);

        PathTransition pathTransition = new PathTransition();
        pathTransition.setDuration(Duration.seconds(5));
        pathTransition.setNode(group);
        pathTransition.setPath(path);
        pathTransition.setOrientation(OrientationType.ORTHOGONAL_TO_TANGENT);
```

```
            pathTransition.play();
        }
    }
```

Compile the preceding code and run it. You will see the image of the ball animated around an elliptical path.

Try This Create a Path Animation

In the previous chapters, the "Try This" sections have focused on added functionality that may not have been directly covered in the chapter. However, the skills covered in this chapter are so important that this section will focus on enhancing these skills.

Create a new project and add an image or shape to it. Then, try creating your own path along which you will animate the image. Experiment with paths of different sizes and lengths. Adjust the speed of your Timelines to change the feel of the animation.

The more you are comfortable with the animation capabilities of JavaFX, the better your applications will be.

Chapter 9 Self Test

1. Why is timing important to animation?

2. What controls the timer in JavaFX animation?

3. True or false? A Timeline contains a child collection of KeyFrames.

4. How do you start the Timeline?

5. True or false? A keyframe is a point at which you want one or more keyvalues to be set to defined values.

6. Which property of Animation sets the number of times a Timeline executes?

7. What is the purpose of ArcTo?

8. A path is created from a group of what?

9. What builder class is used to create an animation from a path?

10. Which PathTransition.OrientationType will change the orientation of the node as it moves along the path?

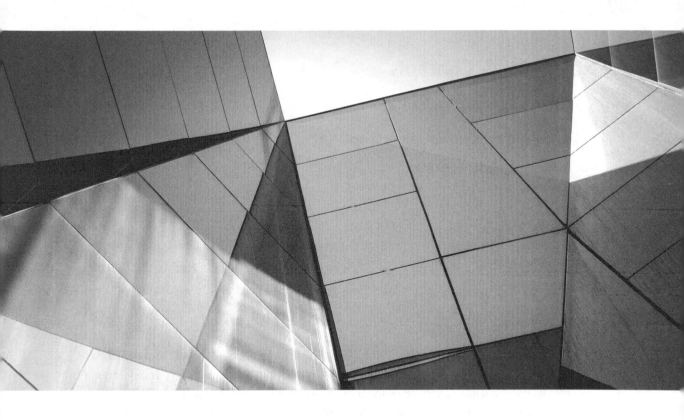

Chapter 10
Using Events

Key Skills & Concepts

- Reacting to mouse events

- Using anonymous inner classes

- Trapping key events

This chapter introduces you to JavaFX events. The concepts that are required when working with events are key in producing rich, interactive applications. Events allow your application to respond to the actions of the user.

What Are Events?

Events provide a way to interact with your users in JavaFX. As a developer, you can use many types of events to enable your users to interact with and react to your environment. Events can be fired as a result of the user interacting in some way with your environment, and you can register listeners for these events and write actions using the data associated with the events.

In this chapter you discover and utilize two common sets of events: mouse events and keyboard events.

Mouse Events

A mouse event is the generic term for the action of any pointer-style input. The provider of this input does not necessarily have to be a physical mouse. Any device that moves a pointer across an environment will generate a mouse event. A mouse, stylus, track ball, track pad, or any other navigational tool will generate a mouse event if it moves your pointer around your JavaFX environment.

Here's a list of the properties of type EventHandler that generate mouse events:

- onMouseClicked

- onMousePressed

- onMouseReleased

- onMouseDragged

- onMouseDragEntered

- onMouseDragExited
- onMouseDragOver
- onMouseDragReleased
- onMouseEntered
- onMouseExited
- onMouseMoved

Although some of these actions may be named descriptively enough for you to figure out what action they listen to, some have similar and confusing names. Therefore, let's clear up any confusion by describing what each action is before we dive into building code around them:

- **onMouseClicked**   This property is used if a full mouse click is detected (the user presses and releases the mouse button).
- **onMousePressed**   This property is used when the user presses the mouse button. The user does not have to release the button to fire this event, like onMouseClick.
- **onMouseReleased**   This property is used for the second half of the onMouseClick event. This property is used when a mouse button is released.
- **onMouseDrag***   These properties are used when a mouse button is held down and the mouse is moved. Mouse-drag-related event objects include the x and y position of the mouse.
- **onMouseEntered**   This property is used when the mouse pointer enters the node to which the event is attached.
- **onMouseExited**   This property is used when the mouse pointer exits the node to which the event is attached.
- **onMouseMoved**   This property is used when the mouse is moved within the borders of the given node.

JavaFX recognizes the completion of the onMouseReleased event as the logical conclusion of a mouse-clicked event. However, if you move the mouse between the time you press the mouse button and release it (that is, perform an intentional or unintentional mouse drag), you will fire the following events in order:

- Mouse pressed
- Mouse dragged
- Mouse released

In this case, no mouse-clicked event is fired. Because other events are fired between the press and the release, JavaFX does not fire a mouse-clicked event.

Note that "mouse clicked" is a specific event that encapsulates a contiguous pair of mouse-pressed and mouse-released events. If any events are fired between "mouse pressed" and "mouse released," the action is no longer considered a mouse-clicked event.

Why then does mouse pressed still fire in both scenarios? Because JavaFX cannot predict what will happen after the mouse-pressed event. It cannot say whether the action will be a mouse-clicked or mouse-released event until the action is completed; therefore, onMousePressed will always fire.

Now that you understand when each event should fire, let's discuss how you register listeners for them.

The onMouse* properties are inherited from Node. Anything that inherits from Node will be able to register listeners for and receive these events. Therefore, all the shapes, buttons, labels, and text boxes that you can add to a Scene will be able to consume these events and let you perform actions based on them.

TIP

Create a new, empty JavaFX app named **Chapter10** to try the following examples.

You should have a new, empty file that looks like this:

```
package Chapter10;

import javafx.application.Application;
import javafx.scene.Scene;
import javafx.scene.layout.StackPane;
import javafx.stage.Stage;

/**
 *
 * @author J F DiMarzio
 */
public class Chapter10 extends Application {

    /**
     * @param args the command line arguments
     */
    public static void main(String[] args) {
        launch(args);
    }

    @Override
    public void start(Stage primaryStage) {
```

```
        StackPane root = new StackPane();

        primaryStage.setScene(new Scene(root, 300, 250));
        primaryStage.show();
    }
}
```

Now, add a circle to the Scene. This circle will be the node we use to consume our mouse events. Finally, add a label to display the events. Your code should look like this:

TIP

For more information about creating circles, refer to Chapter 4.

```java
package Chapter10;

import javafx.application.Application;
import javafx.scene.Group;
import javafx.scene.Scene;
import javafx.scene.control.Label;
import javafx.scene.paint.Color;
import javafx.scene.shape.Circle;
import javafx.stage.Stage;

/**
 *
 * @author J F DiMarzio
 */
public class Chapter10 extends Application {

    /**
     * @param args the command line arguments
     */
    public static void main(String[] args) {
        launch(args);
    }

    @Override
    public void start(Stage primaryStage) {
        Group group = new Group();
        Scene scene = new Scene(group);
        primaryStage.setHeight(350);
        primaryStage.setWidth(350);

        Circle circle = new Circle();
        Label label = new Label();

        circle.setCenterX(150);
        circle.setCenterY(150);
```

```
        circle.setRadius(50);
        circle.setFill(Color.BLUE);

        label.setText("Test");
        group.getChildren().add(circle);
        group.getChildren().add(label);
        primaryStage.setScene(scene);
        primaryStage.show();
    }
}
```

You can now use a convenience method and an anonymous inner class to handle a mouse event—in this case, you will use the onMousePressed event. The purpose of the anonymous inner class is to immediately perform an action when the event is fired. The class will encapsulate all the logic you want to perform when a specific event is fired. In this example, your anonymous inner class will write the contents of the event to the message variable, which is bound to the label text.

You will use a convenience method called setOnMousePressed() to register your anonymous class as a listener for the onMousePressed event.

The code to register your anonymous class using the convenience method looks like this:

```
circle.setOnMousePressed(new EventHandler<MouseEvent>(){
        });
    }
```

In the anonymous function, you need to override the handle method. Inside the handle method, you can add the code you want to execute when the event is fired. For this example, you are going to write the string form of the event to the Label node:

```
circle.setOnMousePressed(new EventHandler<MouseEvent>(){
            @Override
            public void handle(MouseEvent arg0){
                label.setText(arg0.toString());
            }
        });
    }
```

The logic here is that when onMousePressed is triggered—that is, when the user presses the mouse button within the bounds of the circle node—the event is captured and written out to text of the Label. Replicate this same anonymous class for the onMouseClicked event of the circle node. Your finished code should look like this:

```
package Chapter10;

import javafx.application.Application;
import javafx.event.EventHandler;
```

```java
import javafx.scene.Group;
import javafx.scene.Scene;
import javafx.scene.control.Label;
import javafx.scene.input.MouseEvent;
import javafx.scene.paint.Color;
import javafx.scene.shape.Circle;
import javafx.stage.Stage;

/**
 *
 * @author J F DiMarzio
 */
public class Chapter10 extends Application {

    /**
     * @param args the command line arguments
     */
    public static void main(String[] args) {
        launch(args);
    }

    @Override
    public void start(Stage primaryStage) {
        Group group = new Group();
        Scene scene = new Scene(group);
        primaryStage.setHeight(350);
        primaryStage.setWidth(350);

        Circle circle = new Circle();
        final Label label = new Label();

        circle.setCenterX(150);
        circle.setCenterY(150);
        circle.setRadius(50);
        circle.setFill(Color.BLUE);

        circle.setOnMousePressed(new EventHandler<MouseEvent>(){
            @Override
            public void handle(MouseEvent arg0){
                label.setText(arg0.toString());
            }
        });

        circle.setOnMouseClicked(new EventHandler<MouseEvent>(){
            @Override
            public void handle(MouseEvent arg0){
                label.setText(arg0.toString());
            }
```

```
        });
        label.setText("Test");
        group.getChildren().add(circle);
        group.getChildren().add(label);
        primaryStage.setScene(scene);
        primaryStage.show();
    }
}
```

Compile and run the code. You will see a blue circle on the screen like the one shown in Figure 10-1.

Now, move your mouse into the circle and click the mouse button. This will fire the onMousePressed event of the circle and write the following information to the screen:

```
MouseEvent [source = Circle@10fe9e3, target = Circle@10fe9e3, eventType =
MOUSE_PRESSED, consumed = false, x = 163.0, y = 171.0, button = PRIMARY,
primaryButtonDown]
```

Release the mouse button without moving it. You should see the following information:

```
MouseEvent [source = Circle@10fe9e3, target = Circle@10fe9e3, eventType =
MOUSE_CLICKED, consumed = false, x = 163.0, y = 171.0, button = PRIMARY]
```

This indicates that the onMouseClicked event has fired.

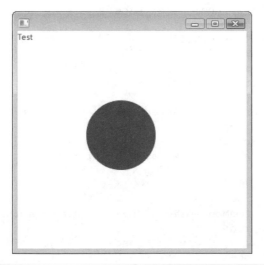

Figure 10-1 A blue circle

Try adding the remaining mouse events to the application (shown next) and testing different scenarios. You should see a large amount of very useful information that you can act upon in your applications.

```java
package Chapter10;

import javafx.application.Application;
import javafx.event.EventHandler;
import javafx.scene.Group;
import javafx.scene.Scene;
import javafx.scene.control.Label;
import javafx.scene.input.MouseEvent;
import javafx.scene.paint.Color;
import javafx.scene.shape.Circle;
import javafx.stage.Stage;

/**
 *
 * @author J F DiMarzio
 */
public class Chapter10 extends Application {

    /**
     * @param args the command line arguments
     */
    public static void main(String[] args) {
        launch(args);
    }

    @Override
    public void start(Stage primaryStage) {
        Group group = new Group();
        Scene scene = new Scene(group);
        primaryStage.setHeight(350);
        primaryStage.setWidth(350);

        Circle circle = new Circle();
        final Label label = new Label();

        circle.setCenterX(150);
        circle.setCenterY(150);
        circle.setRadius(50);
        circle.setFill(Color.BLUE);

        circle.setOnMousePressed(new EventHandler<MouseEvent>(){
            @Override
            public void handle(MouseEvent arg0){
                label.setText(arg0.toString());
```

```
        }
    });

    circle.setOnMouseClicked(new EventHandler<MouseEvent>(){
        @Override
        public void handle(MouseEvent arg0){
            label.setText(arg0.toString());
        }
    });

    circle.setOnMouseDragEntered(new EventHandler<MouseEvent>(){
        @Override
        public void handle(MouseEvent arg0){
            label.setText(arg0.toString());
        }
    });
    circle.setOnMouseDragExited(new EventHandler<MouseEvent>(){
        @Override
        public void handle(MouseEvent arg0){
            label.setText(arg0.toString());
        }
    });
    circle.setOnMouseDragOver(new EventHandler<MouseEvent>(){
        @Override
        public void handle(MouseEvent arg0){
            label.setText(arg0.toString());
        }
    });
    circle.setOnMouseDragReleased(new EventHandler<MouseEvent>(){
        @Override
        public void handle(MouseEvent arg0){
            label.setText(arg0.toString());
        }
    });
    circle.setOnMouseDragged(new EventHandler<MouseEvent>(){
        @Override
        public void handle(MouseEvent arg0){
            label.setText(arg0.toString());
        }
    });
    circle.setOnMouseEntered(new EventHandler<MouseEvent>(){
        @Override
        public void handle(MouseEvent arg0){
            label.setText(arg0.toString());
        }
    });
    circle.setOnMouseExited(new EventHandler<MouseEvent>(){
        @Override
```

```
            public void handle(MouseEvent arg0){
                label.setText(arg0.toString());
            }
        });
        circle.setOnMouseMoved(new EventHandler<MouseEvent>(){
            @Override
            public void handle(MouseEvent arg0){
                label.setText(arg0.toString());
            }
        });
        circle.setOnMouseReleased(new EventHandler<MouseEvent>(){
            @Override
            public void handle(MouseEvent arg0){
                label.setText(arg0.toString());
            }
        });

        label.setText("Test");
        group.getChildren().add(circle);
        group.getChildren().add(label);
        primaryStage.setScene(scene);
        primaryStage.show();
    }
}
```

TIP

Keep in mind that the onMouse* events are inherited from Node. The major implication of this is that Stage and Scene do not inherit from Node. Therefore, you can only consume these events as they occur within Node on the Scene.

Another type of event you can consume is a key event. The following section goes over how to register listeners for, and use, key events.

Key Events

A key event, as the name suggests, is fired when the user interacts with the keyboard. Capturing these keyboard events can be very useful. For example, you could write an application that allows the user to move objects around the Scene with the arrow keys or to stop some animation using the ESC key. Either way, consuming key events can be very useful in your JavaFX apps.

The key event properties are also inherited from Node. Therefore, like the onMouse* properties, only nodes and the Scene can consume key events. The three onKey* properties are onKeyPressed, onKeyReleased, and onKeyTyped. When a user interacts with the keyboard (or keypad for mobile users), the event handlers are called in this order:

- onKeyPressed
- onKeyTyped
- onKeyReleased

Modify your .java file from the last section to listen for these events. The code in your app should look like this when you are finished:

```java
package Chapter10;

import javafx.application.Application;
import javafx.event.EventHandler;
import javafx.scene.Group;
import javafx.scene.Scene;
import javafx.scene.control.Label;
import javafx.scene.input.KeyEvent;
import javafx.scene.paint.Color;
import javafx.scene.shape.Circle;
import javafx.stage.Stage;

/**
 *
 * @author J F DiMarzio
 */
public class Chapter10 extends Application {

    /**
     * @param args the command line arguments
     */
    public static void main(String[] args) {
        launch(args);
    }

    @Override
    public void start(Stage primaryStage) {
        Group group = new Group();
        Scene scene = new Scene(group);
        primaryStage.setHeight(350);
        primaryStage.setWidth(500);

        Circle circle = new Circle();
        final Label label = new Label();
```

```
circle.setCenterX(150);
circle.setCenterY(150);
circle.setRadius(50);
circle.setFill(Color.BLUE);

circle.setOnKeyPressed(new EventHandler<KeyEvent>(){
    @Override
    public void handle(KeyEvent arg0){
        label.setText(arg0.toString());
    }
});
circle.setOnKeyReleased(new EventHandler<KeyEvent>(){
    @Override
    public void handle(KeyEvent arg0){
        label.setText(arg0.toString());
    }
});    .

circle.setOnKeyTyped(new EventHandler<KeyEvent>(){
    @Override
    public void handle(KeyEvent arg0){
        label.setText(arg0.toString());
    }
});
circle.setFocusTraversable(true);

label.setText("Test");
group.getChildren().add(circle);
group.getChildren().add(label);
primaryStage.setScene(scene);
primaryStage.show();
    }
}
```

If you look carefully at the code, you will notice one slight difference in the properties of the Circle node. To get this example to function correctly, a property named focusTraversable needs to be set. The focusTraversable property lets the circle accept the focus of the Scene's action. Without this property being set, JavaFX would not be able to tell what node you are interacting with when you type on the keyboard.

TIP

The focusTraversable property also allows focus to be passed between nodes. If you need a user to be able to move focus from node to node, set focusTraversable to true on both nodes.

With the app compiled and running, click on the circle and then press the number 2 on the keyboard. You should see the following (if you resize the window):

```
KeyEvent [source = Circle@1f77d1c, target = Circle@1f77d1c, eventType =
KEY_PRESSED, consumed = false, character = , text = 2, code = DIGIT2]

KeyEvent [source = Circle@1f77d1c, target = Circle@1f77d1c, eventType =
KEY_TYPED, consumed = false, character = 2, text = , code = UNDEFINED]

KeyEvent [source = Circle@1f77d1c, target = Circle@1f77d1c, eventType =
KEY_RELEASED, consumed = false, character =,  text = 2, code = DIGIT2]
```

Take notice of the character property of the KeyEvent. This property is only available on onKeyTyped. Therefore, if you are using just the character property, you will only see it on onKeyTyped. Now press the up arrow in the emulator and compare the outputs:

```
KeyEvent [source = Circle@914cd5, target = Circle@914cd5, eventType =
KEY_PRESSED, consumed = false, character = , text = , code = UP]

KeyEvent [source = Circle@914cd5, target = Circle@914cd5, eventType =
KEY_RELEASED, consumed = false, character = , text = , code = UP]
```

Notice that the directional arrows do not fire the onKeyTyped event. They will only fire the onKeyPressed and onKeyReleased events.

```
System.out.println(arg0.toString())
```

It is very important to note what events are fired and in what order. This will make your job easier when you are trying to handle user input.

Ask the Expert

Q: What is the importance of the onMouse and onKey events?

A: Using the events described in this chapter is one of the best ways you have to let the user interact with your application. Inevitably, you will need to create an application that requires some level of user interaction. Being able to react to onMouse and onKey events is one of your greatest tools for gathering information from your users.

Chapter 10 Self Test

1. True or false? The onMouse* properties are properties of the Node class.

2. When is onMouseEntered fired?

3. True or false? The mouse-released listener method will be called when the mouse is dragged.

4. True or false? Any class that inherits from Node can register listeners for mouse events.

5. When events are used, what is the purpose of an anonymous inner class?

6. Which mouse event listener is called when the mouse pointer exits the node to which the event listener is attached?

7. What three events listener methods are called when the user interacts with the keyboard?

8. In what order are the key event listener methods called?

9. What property will allow a node to accept focus?

10. True or false? The navigational buttons will fire the onKeyTyped event.

Chapter 11
Custom Nodes
and Subclassing

Key Skills & Concepts

- Subclassing Node
- Creating a custom node
- Overriding default Node methods

JavaFX comes with many great tools. Throughout this book you have learned about shapes, effects, and methods—to name a few. However, what if you find that the nodes in JavaFX do not quite fit what you need? There is another way to get what you need from JavaFX: You can always make a node that does exactly what you need. This can be by subclassing an existing node or by creating an entirely new one. In this chapter you learn about both methods for getting precisely what you need out of JavaFX.

First, let's discuss subclassing an existing node.

Subclassing Node

Before you can learn about overriding methods from Node, a critical question needs to be answered: What is overriding?

Classes, such as Node and Button, contain methods and properties. You as a developer can take these methods and change their default actions to whatever you want. For example, let's say you have a Dog class with a method called displayBreed(), as shown here:

```
public class Dog{
 public void displayBreed(){      System.out.println("Chihuahua");
 }
}
```

You can extend this class and override the displayBreed() method to say something different, as follows:

```
public class MyDog extends Dog {

@Override
public void displayBreed(){
      System.out.println("Elkhound");
 }
}
public class YourDog extends Dog{
}
```

In this example, a call to Dog.displayBreed() would print the line "Chihuahua." A call to YourDog.displayBreed() would also print "Chihuahua." However, because MyDog overrides the displayBreed() method, a call to MyDog.getBreed() would print "Elkhound."

Using overriding, you can create nodes with new or expanded functionality. In the following section you create a new Button by subclassing the default JavaFX button class and overriding some of the default functionality. This Button will be a small round button that can be created to display either a plus sign (+) or a minus sign (–). The completed button will be used in another project in the next chapter.

To prepare for this exercise, create a new JavaFX Application and name the project **Chapter11**. The Chapter11.java file should appear as follows—after you remove the Hello World code:

```
package Chapter11;

import javafx.application.Application;
import javafx.scene.Scene;
import javafx.scene.layout.StackPane;
import javafx.stage.Stage;

/**
 *
 * @author J F DiMarzio
 */
public class Chapter11 extends Application {

    /**
     * @param args the command line arguments
     */
    public static void main(String[] args) {
        launch(args);
    }

    @Override
    public void start(Stage primaryStage) {
        StackPane root = new StackPane();
        root.getChildren().add(btn);
        primaryStage.setScene(new Scene(root, 300, 250));
        primaryStage.show();
    }
}
```

Creating a RoundButton

In this section you are going to create multiple files that, together, will give you a new RoundButton that can be used in other projects.

Now create a new file by right-clicking on the Chapter11 package and selecting New | Java Interface. Set the Class Name to RoundButtonAPI. This will be the interface that provides a new method to your RoundButton class (which you will create later in this section).

In the RoundButtonAPI interface, you are going to create two public integers representing the type of the button that will be created and a method named setType() that will accept one of the aforementioned integers. Your completed interface should look like this:

```
package Chapter11;

/**
 *
 * @author J F DiMarzio
 */
public interface RoundButtonAPI {
    public static final int PLUS = 1;
    public static final int MINUS = 2;

    public void setType(int type);
}
```

You can now create a new class that will implement this interface and use it in creating the round button. Right-click on your package and add a new Java class named RoundButton. You should have an empty class that appears as follows:

```
package Chapter11;

/**
 *
 * @author J F DiMarzio
 */
public class RoundButton {

}
```

The first step is to make RountButton a button. You want this class to have all of the functionality and properties of a standard button; you just want to enhance it slightly. Therefore, you need to have your class extend javafx.scene.control.Button. To add the functionality of specifying the type of the button, implement the interface that you just created, like so:

```
package Chapter11;

/**
```

```
*
* @author J F DiMarzio
*/
public class RoundButton extends
javafx.scene.control.Button implements RoundButtonAPI{

}
```

NOTE
At this point, assuming that you are using NetBeans, you may get a prompt from the IDE that you need to add some unimplemented methods from RoundButtonAPI. Let NetBeans implement the setType() method for you; otherwise, you will need to implement it yourself following the code example.

If you were to just stop here, you would have a fully functional button named RoundButton. You would be able to use this button in your application as you would any button. But stopping here would not give you an actual round button. You would just have a copy of Button named RoundButton.

This button works with so little code because you are telling it to extend the functionality of Button into RoundButton. Therefore, all the methods and properties of Button will now be a part of RoundButton. In its current state, the round button looks and acts exactly like Button.

However, for this example you want to create a button that is round. Therefore, you need to add code to the RoundButton class that will make the button round. This is achieved by setting the clip property of Button in RoundButton to always make the button round.

To override the setType method, add the following code to set the button's clip to a circle:

```
@Override
  public void setType(int type) {
      Circle roundButtonClip = new Circle();
      roundButtonClip.setCenterX(18);
      roundButtonClip.setCenterY(12);
      roundButtonClip.setRadius(8);
      this.setClip(roundButtonClip);
  }
```

Next, add a quick if statement to determine whether the button is of type 1 or 2. The purpose of this is to let the user choose whether the button text should be + or –. A buttonType of 1 would set the text of RoundButton to +, whereas a buttonType of 2 would set the text of RoundButton to –.

```
@Override
    public void setType(int type) {
        Circle roundButtonClip = new Circle();
        roundButtonClip.setCenterX(18);
        roundButtonClip.setCenterY(12);
        roundButtonClip.setRadius(8);
        this.setClip(roundButtonClip);

        if(type == 1){
            this.setText(" +");
        }else{
            this.setText(" -");
        }
    }
}
```

The finished class should look like this:

```
package Chapter11;

import javafx.scene.shape.Circle;


/**
 *
 * @author J F DiMarzio
 */
public final class RoundButton extends
javafx.scene.control.Button implements
RoundButtonAPI{

    @Override
    public void setType(int type) {
        Circle roundButtonClip = new Circle();
        roundButtonClip.setCenterX(18);
        roundButtonClip.setCenterY(12);
        roundButtonClip.setRadius(8);
        this.setClip(roundButtonClip);

        if(type == 1){
            this.setText(" +");
        }else{
            this.setText(" -");
        }
    }

    public RoundButton(){
    }
```

```
    public RoundButton(int type)
    {
        this.setType(type);
    }
}
```

Unlike the other examples you have built in this book, you cannot compile and run this class as it is. What you have right now is a class that can be called from another application. Now you can add some code to Chapter11.java and use your new button. Your Chapter11.java file currently should look like this:

```
package Chapter11;

import javafx.application.Application;
import javafx.scene.Scene;
import javafx.scene.layout.StackPane;
import javafx.stage.Stage;

/**
 *
 * @author J F DiMarzio
 */
public class Chapter11 extends Application {

    /**
     * @param args the command line arguments
     */
    public static void main(String[] args) {
        launch(args);
    }

    @Override
    public void start(Stage primaryStage) {
        StackPane root = new StackPane();

        primaryStage.setScene(new Scene(root, 300, 250));
        primaryStage.show();
    }
}
```

Now all you have to do is call your new RoundButton from the content start() method. This is very easy to do. You can call RoundButton just as you would any other node. Remember to pass the button type to the constructor:

```
RoundButton btn = new RoundButton(RoundButton.PLUS);
```

This will create a round button with + as the text. The full Chapter11.java looks like this:

```java
package Chapter11;

import javafx.application.Application;
import javafx.scene.Scene;
import javafx.scene.layout.StackPane;
import javafx.stage.Stage;

/**
 *
 * @author J F DiMarzio
 */
public class Chapter11 extends Application {

    /**
     * @param args the command line arguments
     */
    public static void main(String[] args) {
        launch(args);
    }

    @Override
    public void start(Stage primaryStage) {

        RoundButton btn = new RoundButton(RoundButton.PLUS);

        StackPane root = new StackPane();
        root.getChildren().add(btn);
        primaryStage.setScene(new Scene(root, 300, 250));
        primaryStage.show();
    }
}
```

NOTE

Some nodes, this RoundButton included, render differently on the Mac and PC. Take this into consideration when comparing your results with those in the images in this chapter.

Compile and run this application. You will see a round button like the one shown in Figure 11-1.

To see one of the advantages of subclassing an existing node to create your own, add a second button with a buttonType of 0, as follows. Notice that the StackPanel has been traded out for an HBox. This will allow you to place the buttons next to each other, rather than overlay them.

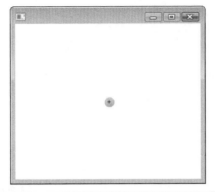

Figure 11-1   A RoundButton

```java
package Chapter11;

import javafx.application.Application;
import javafx.scene.Scene;
import javafx.scene.layout.HBox;
import javafx.stage.Stage;

/**
 *
 * @author J F DiMarzio
 */
public class Chapter11 extends Application {

    /**
     * @param args the command line arguments
     */
    public static void main(String[] args) {
        launch(args);
    }

    @Override
    public void start(Stage primaryStage) {

        RoundButton btn = new RoundButton(RoundButton.PLUS);
        RoundButton btn2 = new RoundButton(RoundButton.MINUS);

        HBox root = new HBox();
        root.getChildren().add(btn);
        root.getChildren().add(btn2);

        primaryStage.setScene(new Scene(root, 300, 250));
        primaryStage.show();
    }
}
```

Figure 11-2 A second RoundButton

Compile and run this application to produce the two buttons shown in Figure 11-2.

It becomes very easy now to add multiple instances of nodes. If you know you will be adding multiple instances of a node, it is best to use this technique.

Try This   Create Your Own Shapes

In this chapter you used a mask to create a round button. For an added challenge, try this exercise to expand your knowledge. Create a new project and, using the skills you gained from this chapter, create different shapes of different nodes. Experiment with triangular buttons, rounded-corner text boxes, and other nontraditional shapes. Then, using the RoundButton example, create a custom node of your new shape and use it in a Scene.

In the next chapter you will learn how to embed music and videos in your scripts.

Chapter 11 Self Test

1. What process lets you take methods from one class and change their default behavior?

2. When you're creating a class, what keyword forces your class to inherit the methods and properties of another?

3. In the following example, what will a call to YourDog.displayBreed print?

```
public class MyDog extends Dog {
@Override
public void displayBreed(){
     System.out.println("Elkhound");
  }
}
public class YourDog extends Dog{
  }
```

4. True or false? Ensuring that your files are all in the same package will make referencing them easier.

5. True or false? The process of inheriting from another class is known as subclassing.

6. What keyword do you use to implement an interface?

7. True or false? You instantiate custom created nodes the same way you would instantiate a standard one.

8. What is the purpose of an HBox?

9. What annotation, beginning with @, can be used when you change the default functionality of an inherited method?

10. True or false? Creating an API interface for your custom classes is a good coding procedure.

Chapter 12
Working with WebView

Key Skills & Concepts

- Rendering HTML
- Communicating between JavaScript and JavaFX

With the abundance of business and sites built around streaming media, it is only natural that JavaFX allow you to take full advantage of embedded video and audio media. In the past, programming an application to play any kind of media meant hours of writing controls, finding the right codecs for the files you wanted to play, and writing parsers to read the media files. It was long and arduous work that you would really only attempt if you were completely confident in your abilities as a programmer.

Rather than require you to link directly to the media that you want to stream through JavaFX, there is a much more robust solution waiting for you. JavaFX includes a WebView. The JavaFX WebView is based on the ubiquitous, open-source WebKit—thus allowing you to display HTML5 and use CSS and JavaScript.

In the first section of this chapter you will work with displaying HTML using WebView. However, before you begin, you need to create a new, empty JavaFX project named **Chapter12**. Your script should appear as follows:

```
package chapter12;

import javafx.application.Application;
import javafx.scene.Scene;
import javafx.scene.layout.StackPane;
import javafx.stage.Stage;

/**
 *
 * @author J F DiMarzio
 */
public class Chapter12 extends Application {

    /**
     * @param args the command line arguments
     */
    public static void main(String[] args) {
        launch(args);
    }
```

```
      @Override
      public void start(Stage primaryStage) {

      }
}
```

You also need to create a second empty JavaFX class named HTMLLoader. This class will hold the setup for the WebView. You will be adding to this second file throughout the chapter. Name the file **HTMLLoader.class** and then set it up as follows:

```
package chapter12;

/**
 *
 * @author J F DiMarzio
 */
public class HTMLLoader extends Region {

}
```

Let's add some code to the HTMLLoader to display a web page.

Rendering HTML

The WebView node is based on the open-source WebKit architecture. You can easily use a WebView in your JavaFX application to render HTML. The example in this section will render a website in a WebView.

TIP
Notice that the HTMLLoader class extends Region. Extending Region allows our class to contain children nodes and to apply CSS to those nodes.

Let's start by instantiating a WebView and a WebEngine. The WebEngine class allows you management over the WebView. You will use the WebEngine to apply style sheets, point to web pages, and provide a communication path between JavaScript and Java (later in the book).

Import the following packages to your HTMLLoader class:

```
import javafx.scene.web.WebEngine;
import javafx.scene.web.WebView;
```

Next, instantiate the WebView and WebEngine:

```
public class HTMLLoader extends Region {
```

```
final WebView browser = new WebView();
final WebEngine webEngine = browser.getEngine();

...

}
```

The rest of the work for the HTMLLoader will be performed in the constructor. Create a constructor for the HTMLLoader class:

```
public HTMLLoader() {
}
```

Within the constructor, use the load() method of the WebEngine to load the jfdimarzio .com website. Then, using the getChildren().add() method of the HTMLLoader, add the WebView to the HTMLLoader/Region:

```
public HTMLLoader() {
    webEngine.load("http://jfdimarzio.com");
     getChildren().add(browser);

  }
```

Finally, instantiate an HTMLLoader and add it to your Scene:

```
public void start(Stage primaryStage) {

    primaryStage.setTitle("WebView");
    Scene scene;
    scene = new Scene(new HTMLLoader(),800,600);
    primaryStage.setScene(scene);
    primaryStage.show();
}
```

Compile and run the code for this chapter and you should see a JavaFX application with a rendered web page, as shown in Figure 12-1.

Communicating Between JavaScript and JavaFX

In the previous section you used the WebEngine to manage a WebView. The WebEngine can perform other functions as well. One of the more useful functions that the WebEngine can perform is to facilitate the communication between JavaScript and JavaFX.

This is not to say that the WebEngine can arbitrarily execute JavaScript on an unsuspecting page. Rather, the WebEngine can be used to enhance existing functionality on a page. For example, the WebEngine can be used to execute JavaScript against a page. This by itself is not terribly exciting. However, WebEngine also facilitates the opposite behavior as well—you can communicate from JavaScript to JavaFX.

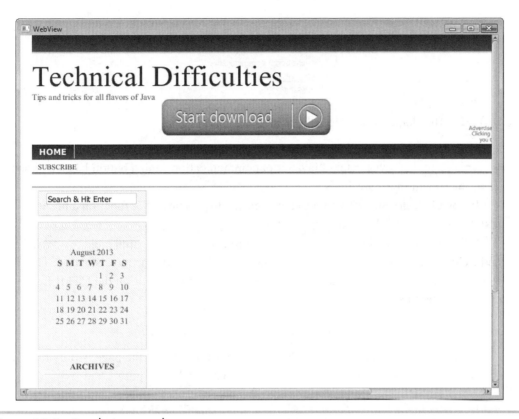

Figure 12-1 Rendering a web page

First, let's examine JavaFX-to-JavaScript communication. Take a simple HTML page with a JavaScript function like that found at jfdimarzio.com/test.html, shown here:

```
<!DOCTYPE html>
<html>
<head>
<script>
function displayJavaFX()
{
document.getElementById("javafx").innerHTML='JavaFX to ';
}
</script>
</head>
<body>
<h1>Chapter 12</h1>
<p id="javafx"></p>
<p>JavaScript communication</p>
<p><button type="button" onclick="displayJavaFX()">Show Text</button></p>
</body>
</html>
```

Chapter 12

JavaScript communication

Figure 12-2 The demo page before JavaScript execution

This page displays the text "JavaScript communication" and a button labeled "Show Text," as shown in Figure 12-2.

If you click the Show Text button, it fires the displayJavaFX() function and shows the text "JavaFX to," as shown in Figure 12-3.

Using the WebEngine, you can load the jfdimarzio.com/test.html page in a WebView and execute the showJavaFX() function—without clicking on the page's button. The first step is to load the page into the WebView using the WebEngine. Edit the HTMLLoader to display the text page:

```
webEngine.load("http://jfdimarzio.com/test.html");
```

Before you can execute the JavaScript, you must make sure the page is fully loaded by the WebView. Luckily you can invoke a listener just for this purpose:

```
webEngine.getLoadWorker().stateProperty().addListener(
        new ChangeListener<State>() {
            @Override
            public void changed(ObservableValue<? extends State> ov,
            State oldState, State newState) {
                if (newState == State.SUCCEEDED) {
                    //Execute JavaScript here
                }
            }
        }
);
```

Chapter 12

JavaFX to

JavaScript communication

Show Text

Figure 12-3 The demo page after the JavaScript execution

Within the test, use the executeScript() method of the WebEngine to call the displayJavaFX() function:

```
webEngine.getLoadWorker().stateProperty().addListener(
        new ChangeListener<State>() {
            @Override
            public void changed(ObservableValue<? extends State> ov,
            State oldState, State newState) {
                if (newState == State.SUCCEEDED) {
webEngine.executeScript("displayJavaFX()");
                }
            }
        }
);
```

The full code of the HTMLLoader should appear as follows:

```
public class HTMLLoader extends Region {

    final WebView browser = new WebView();
    final WebEngine webEngine = browser.getEngine();

    public HTMLLoader() {
        webEngine.load("http://jfdimarzio.com/test.html");

        webEngine.getLoadWorker().stateProperty().addListener(
            new ChangeListener<State>() {
                @Override
                public void changed(ObservableValue<? extends State> ov,
                    State oldState, State newState) {
                    if (newState == State.SUCCEEDED) {
                        webEngine.executeScript("displayJavaFX()");
                    }
                }
            }
        );

    }

}
```

Compile and run the code. The page should load and the script execute as shown in Figure 12-4.

Earlier in this section I stated that the WebEngine not only can allow for JavaFX-to-JavaScript communications but also can facilitate JavaScript-to-JavaFX communication. In the following example, you will further modify the HTMLLoader app to show how the WebEngine facilitates JavaScript-to-JavaFX communications.

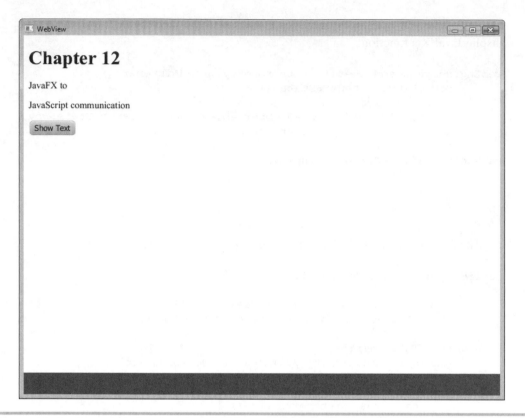

Figure 12-4 Executing the showJavaFX() function from JavaFX

Modify the call to the executeScript() method to throw up a JavaScript alert:

```
webEngine.executeScript("alert('Hello World');");
```

For security, JavaFX will not pass the alert pop-up to the application. Running this application now will not give any indication that a JavaScript function was executed. However, JavaFX provides a rather suitable solution. You can establish a line of communication from JavaScript to JavaFX, listen for the execution of the alert, and intercept the contents of it—to do with as you please.

Let's set up an example where the contents of the alert are written to a label on the JavaFX app. The following modification to HTMLLoader sets up a toolbar at the bottom of the application with a label:

```
public class HTMLLoader extends Region {

    final WebView browser = new WebView();
    final WebEngine webEngine = browser.getEngine();
    HBox toolbar;
```

```
        public HTMLLoader() {
            webEngine.load("http://jfdimarzio.com/test.html");
            final Label lblHello = new Label();

            webEngine.getLoadWorker().stateProperty().addListener(
                new ChangeListener<State>() {
                    @Override
                    public void changed(ObservableValue<? extends State> ov,
                        State oldState, State newState) {
                            if (newState == State.SUCCEEDED) {
                                webEngine.executeScript("alert('Hello World');");
                            }
                        }
                    }
            );
            toolbar = new HBox();
            toolbar.setPadding(new Insets(10, 10, 10, 10));
            toolbar.setSpacing(10);
            toolbar.setStyle("-fx-background-color: #336699");
            toolbar.getChildren().add(lblHello);

            getChildren().add(browser);
            getChildren().add(toolbar);

        }
        private Node createSpacer() {
            Region spacer = new Region();
            HBox.setHgrow(spacer, Priority.ALWAYS);
            return spacer;
        }

        @Override protected void layoutChildren() {
            double w = getWidth();
            double h = getHeight();
            double toolbarHeight = toolbar.prefHeight(w);
            layoutInArea(browser,0,0,w,h,0, HPos.CENTER, VPos.CENTER);
            layoutInArea(toolbar, 0, h-toolbarHeight, w, toolbarHeight, 0,
HPos.CENTER, VPos.CENTER);
        }

        @Override protected double computePrefWidth(double height) {
            return 800;
        }

        @Override protected double computePrefHeight(double width) {
            return 600;
        }

}
```

The WebEngine provides a setOnAlert() event listener that can be used to listen for
any execution of the JavaScript alert(). Set up a setOnAlert() listener to listen for the Hello
World alert box and write the contents of it to the label.

TIP

Keep in mind, you do not need to have any knowledge of the contents or purpose of the alert() to use this method. Any page that executes an alert() will be intercepted by this listener.

```
webEngine.setOnAlert(new EventHandler<WebEvent<String>>(){
        @Override
        public void handle(WebEvent<String> arg0) {
            lblHello.setText(arg0.getData());
        }
    });
```

Compile and run the new code, and you should see the result of the alert in toolbar at the bottom of the screen, as shown in Figure 12-5.

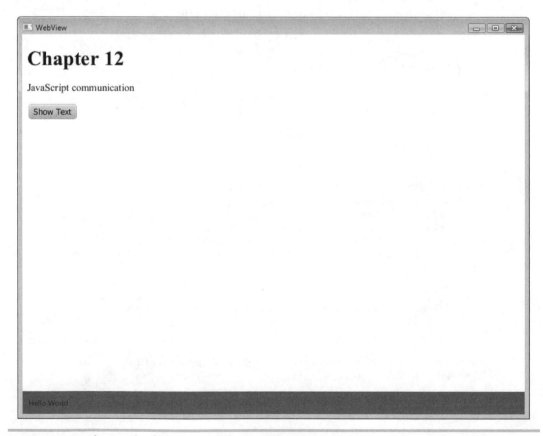

Figure 12-5 The result of JavaScript-to-JavaFX communication

Chapter 12 Self Test

1. What node is used to hold or render a web page in a JavaFX app?

2. What packages contain the nodes needed to work with WebView and WebEngine?

3. What method of the WebEngine is used to load a web page into a WebView?

4. True or false? JavaScript-to-JavaFX communication is prohibited within JavaFX.

5. What method is used to execute a JavaScript against a page loaded in the WebView?

Chapter 13
Style Your JavaFX
with CSS

Key Skills & Concepts

- Adding CSS files to your packages
- Using CSS classes
- Accessing Node properties

In this chapter you learn how to use Cascading Style Sheets (CSS) to easily change the look and feel of your JavaFX applications. If you are not fully aware of what CSS is, this very quick refresher should help.

CSS is a styling language that allows you to separate the styling elements of an object from the object itself. Although CSS was created long before JavaFX, JavaFX includes the ability to use this styling language. In fact, the JavaFX CSS is based on the W3C version 2.1 CSS standard. That means you can create all your objects—or nodes in JavaFX—without any care for their placement, look, or feel. All you have to do is define the functionality of your nodes. Then, either in the style property of the nodes or in a separate file altogether, you can define styles that change the placement, look, and feel of your nodes.

An important feature of CSS you should note here is that all your CSS styles can be contained in a file separate from your .java file. Keeping your code and .css files separate allows you to change your styles—and even change the complete look and feel of your application—without needing to change or recompile your application. What does this mean to you? You can change the look and feel of an application you've designed by modifying the .css file, while leaving your application's code untouched.

Ask the Expert

Q: Is there a difference between the CSS used in JavaFX and the CSS used on web pages?

A: Yes. JavaFX supports new JavaFX-specific elements. It is unclear how many, if any, of the standard CSS elements JavaFX will support in the future.

The remainder of this chapter teaches you how to leverage this very useful tool in your applications. Before you begin, set up a new, empty JavaFX app named **Chapter13**, as follows:

```
package chapter13;

import javafx.application.Application;
import javafx.scene.Scene;
import javafx.scene.layout.StackPane;
import javafx.stage.Stage;

/**
 *
 * @author J F DiMarzio
 */
public class Chapter13 extends Application {

    /**
     * @param args the command line arguments
     */
    public static void main(String[] args) {
        launch(args);
    }

    @Override
    public void start(Stage primaryStage) {

        StackPane root = new StackPane();

        primaryStage.setScene(new Scene(root, 300, 250));
        primaryStage.show();
    }
}
```

In the first section of this chapter, you learn how to add a style sheet to your JavaFX package for use in your script.

Adding a Style Sheet to Your Packages

The first step is to right-click your package name from the Projects view of NetBeans (on the left side of the IDE). Select New | Other from the context menu, which opens the New File Wizard (see Figure 13-1).

In the wizard, you want to select Other from the Categories area and then Cascading Style Sheet from the File Types area, as shown in Figure 13-2.

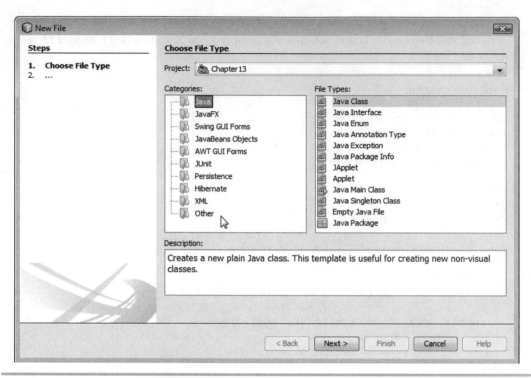

Figure 13-1 The result of selecting New | Other from the context menu

Finally, click the Next button, name your file **default**, and then click the Finish button, as shown in Figure 13-3.

You now have a file named default.css in your list of package files. If it is not open already, open your style sheet. It should appear as follows:

```
/*
    Document    : default
    Created on : Oct 13, 2012, 11:48:53 AM
    Author      : J F DiMarzio
    Description:
        Purpose of the style sheet follows.
*/

root {
    display: block;
}
```

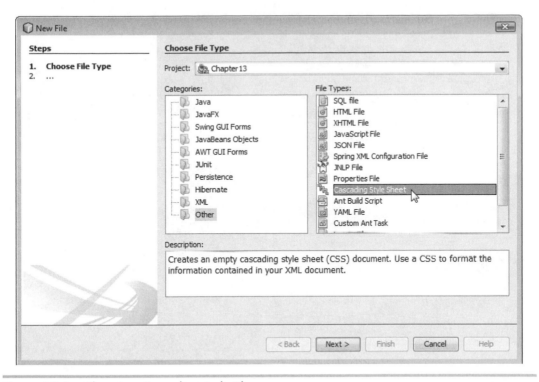

Figure 13-2   Choosing Cascading Style Sheet

Notice how the CSS file contains a comments section, much like your JavaFX files. This comments section is followed by the styles. When you create a new style sheet using the New File Wizard, one style is automatically created for you. This style contains one selector and one declaration. This is a simple style that states that anything in the root is visible.

TIP

Keep in mind, the purpose of this chapter is not to teach you CSS as a language. Rather, you are just learning how to use CSS in relationship to JavaFX. If you need more instruction on CSS and how to use CSS properties, try using one of the many online resources available before you proceed with this chapter.

With the style sheet created and inserted into the working package, you can focus on creating your first style. Next, you create a style that can be applied to the Label nodes in a future JavaFX script.

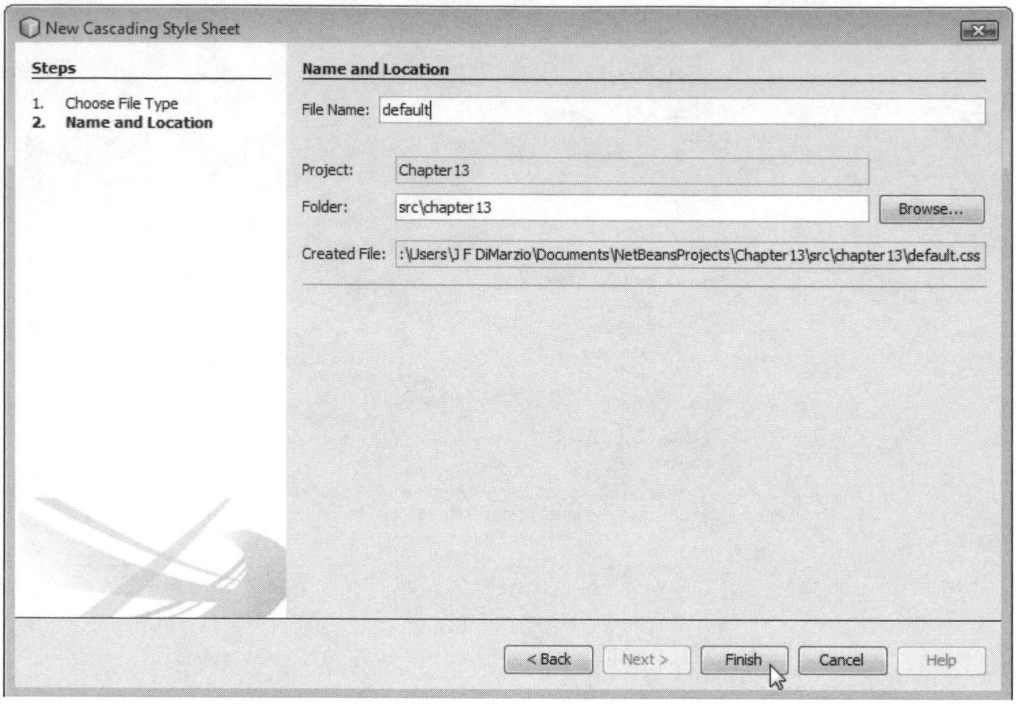

Figure 13-3 Finalizing your file

Creating a Style

JavaFX will automatically recognize any CSS style class created with the name of a node. For example, if you wanted to create a CSS class that applies to all Label nodes, you would create a style class named .label. Let's create a .label class now. You will use this class in your script later.

```
.label{
}
```

In this class, you change the Label node's font color to red and the font to Courier 14 pt. You need to add the correct properties to the style class for changing the font and font color. Luckily, JavaFX also recognize CSS style properties that are written to access Node properties directly.

The Node property for changing the color of a font in a label is textFill. To access this property from the CSS, you need to add "-fx-" as a prefix and separate each word with a hyphen (-). Thus, the style declaration would look like this:

```
.label{
    -fx-text-fill: red;
}
```

This style states that any Label node will have its textFill property set to RED. Let's create one more declaration for the Label node, and then you can apply this style sheet to a script.

To change the font of the Label node, use the –fx-font style, as follows:

```
.label{
    -fx-text-fill: red;
    -fx-font: bold 14pt "Courier";
}
```

In total, this style changes the font of all labels to a red, bold, 14-point Courier. The full CSS file should look like this:

```
/*
    Document    : default
    Created on  : Oct 13, 2012, 11:48:53 AM
    Author      : J F DiMarzio
    Description:
        Purpose of the style sheet follows.
*/

root {
    display: block;
}
.label{
    -fx-text-fill: red;
    -fx-font: bold 14pt "Courier";
}
```

Now let's apply this full CSS file to a JavaFX app.

Using Your Styles

In the previous sections you learned how to create a separate CSS file. You then created a style within that CSS file to be applied to all Label nodes. Let's now open Chapter13.fx and create a label that can use this new CSS file.

First, add a Stage and Scene to your file, as follows:

```
package chapter13;

import javafx.application.Application;
import javafx.scene.Scene;
```

```
import javafx.scene.layout.StackPane;
import javafx.stage.Stage;

/**
 *
 * @author J F DiMarzio
 */
public class Chapter13 extends Application {

    /**
     * @param args the command line arguments
     */
    public static void main(String[] args) {
        launch(args);
    }

    @Override
    public void start(Stage primaryStage) {

        StackPane root = new StackPane();
        primaryStage.setScene(new Scene(root, 300, 250));
        primaryStage.show();
    }
}
```

To use the style sheet in this script, you need to apply it to the root. The root has a property called Stylesheets. Notice that the name of the property is plural. This is because you can apply multiple style sheets to a single item.

Use the property getter and setter to add style sheet, as follows:

```
root.getStylesheets().add(Chapter13.class
    .getResource("default.css").toExternalForm());
```

Now, simply add a Label node to the Scene:

```
package chapter13;

import javafx.application.Application;
import javafx.scene.Scene;
import javafx.scene.control.Label;
import javafx.scene.layout.StackPane;
import javafx.stage.Stage;

/**
 *
 * @author J F DiMarzio
 */
```

```
public class Chapter13 extends Application {

    /**
     * @param args the command line arguments
     */
    public static void main(String[] args) {
        launch(args);
    }

    @Override
    public void start(Stage primaryStage) {
        Label label = new Label();
        label.setText("This is a test");

        StackPanc root - new StackPane();
        root.getChildren().add(label);

root.getStylesheets().add(chapter13.Chapter13.class
    .getResource("default.css").toExternalForm());
        primaryStage.setScene(new Scene(root, 300, 250));
        primaryStage.show();
    }
}
```

Notice that within the code you are not modifying the Label node in any way. Normally this would result in a label with standard black font. However, because you applied the default.css file, the font will end up being red, bold, and Courier.

Compile and run this app. You will see a result like that shown in Figure 13-4.

In the final section of this chapter, you learn about creating style classes that can be applied independent of the node.

Figure 13-4 Label with style applied

Creating Independent Style Classes

Open the default.css file once more. You are going to add a style class to this file that can be applied to any node, regardless of its type. That is, whereas you created a style previously that would only be applied to all labels, you will now create a style class that can be applied to any node you want.

Let's create a class that rotates any node by 90 degrees. Add the following class to your default.css file:

```
.rotate{
    -fx-rotate:90;
}
```

Notice here that the Node property for rotating a node is called rotate. Therefore, the style sheet declaration for this is -fx-rotate. Your full default.css should now look like this:

```
/*
    Document    : default
    Created on  : Oct 13, 2012, 11:48:53 AM
    Author      : J F DiMarzio
    Description:
        Purpose of the style sheet follows.
*/

root{
    display:block;
}

 .label{
    -fx-text-fill: red;
    -fx-font: bold 14pt "Courier";
}
.rotate{
    -fx-rotate:90;
}
```

Now you need to modify Chapter13.java to use this new class.

The .rotate class you just created is an independent class that you need to call specifically if you want to use it—unlike the .label class, which will inherently be applied to all labels. The StyleClass property of a node allows you to specify a class within the current style sheet that you want to apply to the node. Modify the Label code in your Chapter13.java file to include a call to the getter and setter of the StyleClass property:

```
package chapter13;

import javafx.application.Application;
import javafx.scene.Scene;
import javafx.scene.control.Label;
```

```
import javafx.scene.layout.StackPane;
import javafx.stage.Stage;

/**
 *
 * @author J F DiMarzio
 */
public class Chapter13 extends Application {

    /**
     * @param args the command line arguments
     */
    public static void main(String[] args) {
        launch(args);
    }

    @Override
    public void start(Stage primaryStage) {
        Label label = new Label();
        label.setText("This is a test");
label.getStyleClass().add("rotate");

        StackPane root = new StackPane();
        root.getChildren().add(label);
        root.getStylesheets().add(chapter13.Chapter13.class
            .getResource("default.css").toExternalForm());
        primaryStage.setScene(new Scene(root, 300, 250));
        primaryStage.show();
    }
}
```

Compile and run this app, with the new default.css. You will see a change in your label's text, like that shown in Figure 13-5.

Figure 13-5   Label with the .rotate class

Experiment with styles and nodes. Using the examples covered in this chapter, create a style class that changes the position or color of a node.

Chapter 13 Self Test

1. What is Cascading Style Sheets (CSS)?

2. What file extension is used for Cascading Style Sheets?

3. What wizard helps you create and add a CSS to your package?

4. If you use the wizard to create your CSS, what class is added by default?

5. True or false? To create a CSS class that applies to all nodes of a certain type, the name of the class should be the name of the node type in lowercase.

6. What prefix is added to every Node property to call it from a CSS class?

7. What property of Scene will let you apply a style sheet to your script?

8. True or false? You can only add one style sheet to a Scene.

9. What Node property allows you to assign a specific CSS class to a node?

10. True or false? If you have a node with a node-applied CSS class and a styleClass property, the style in the styleClass will override that in the node-applied style.

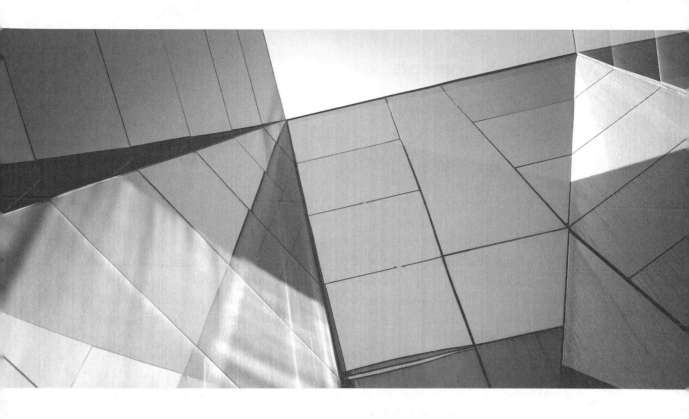

Chapter 14
Embedded Media

Key Skills & Concepts

- Adding video to an app
- Inverse binding
- Using the MediaPlayer

With the abundance of business and sites built around streaming media, it is only natural that JavaFX allow you to take full advantage of video and audio media. In the past, programming an application to play any kind of media meant hours of writing controls, finding the right codecs for the files you wanted to play, and writing parsers to read the media files. It was long and arduous work that you would really only attempt if you were completely confident in your abilities as a programmer.

JavaFX has packaged a few classes that make working with media files as easy as possible. In this chapter you learn about the MediaView and MediaPlayer classes. You use these classes to write apps that display video, play audio, and allow users a level of control over the media they choose to play.

In the first section, you learn how MediaView and MediaPlayer can be used together to play a video file. However, before you begin, you need to create a new, empty JavaFX project named **Chapter14**. Your code should appear as follows:

```
package Chapter14;

import javafx.application.Application;
import javafx.scene.Scene;
import javafx.scene.layout.StackPane;
import javafx.stage.Stage;

/**
 *
 * @author J F DiMarzio
 */
public class Chapter14 extends Application {

    /**
     * @param args the command line arguments
     */
    public static void main(String[] args) {
        launch(args);
    }
```

```
    @Override
    public void start(Stage primaryStage) {

    }
}
```

You also need to create a second empty JavaFX class. This second file will hold a custom node for the playback of media files. You will be adding to this second file throughout the chapter. Name the file **MyMediaViewMyMediaView.class** and set it up as follows:

```
package Chapter14;
import javafx.scene.media.MediaView;

/**
 *
 * @author J F DiMarzio
 */
public class MyMediaViewMyMediaView extends MediaView {

}
```

In the following sections you learn how easy it is to add video files and audio files to your applications.

Playing Video

JavaFX uses the MediaView node to display video to the screen. However, the MediaView is really just a container for a MediaPlayer. The MediaPlayer class is the one that plays the video.

In this section you use a MediaView and a MediaPlayer to play some sample video from within your application. You will be surprised at just how easy JavaFX makes it to play video from a script.

TIP

The sample video used in this section can be downloaded from http://download.oracle .com/. However, we will be streaming it directly from the site.

Let's start by creating a MediaPlayer. After the MediaPlayer is created and some parameters are set, you will add it to a MediaView.

To begin, open your MyMediaView class. The classes needed to work with media files are located in the import javafx.scene.media package. JavaFX does a really good job

Ask the Expert

Q: **What kind of files can the MediaPlayer play?**

A: The quick answer is, if the file is supported by QuickTime on Mac or Windows Media Player on Windows, the MediaPlayer node will be able to handle it. Specific supported file formats include MP3, MP4, and FLV.

of naming everything logically and placing all related classes in common packages. The javafx.scene.media package is no exception.

Import the following class to your MyMediaView file:

```
import javafx.scene.media.MediaPlayer;
```

So why go through the extra step of subclassing MediaPlayer? Although it is true that you could just add the MediaPlayer directly to a MediaView and be done with it, the stock MediaPlayer is very simplistic. As you progress through this chapter, you will be adding functionality to MyMediaView that extends the usability of MediaPlayer.

For now you will set up a stock MediaPlayer, just to show how easy it is to load and play a video file:

```
private MediaPlayer _player;
```

The second thing you will need is a Media object. The Media object represents the source of the media to be played using the MediaPlayer. For this example, you are going to hard-code a sample video file that will be streamed from the Oracle site. This saves you the effort of constantly having to assign this property.

To use the Media class, include the following import statement:

```
import javafx.scene.media.Media;
```

Then add the code to create the Media class:

```
private Media _media;
```

Next, create an empty constructor for MyMediaView:

```
package Chapter14;

import javafx.scene.media.Media;
import javafx.scene.media.MediaPlayer;
```

```
/**
 *
 * @author J F DiMarzio
 */
public class MyMediaView extends javafx.scene.media.MediaView {
    private MediaPlayer _player;
    private Media _media;

    public MyMediaView()
    {
    }
}
```

Within the constructor, you need to instantiate your Media and then instantiate the MediaPlayer with the Media that you want to play:

```
_media = new Media(http://download.oracle.com/ +
        "otndocs/products/javafx/oow2010-2.flv");
_player = new MediaPlayer(_media);
```

You will need to set two properties of the MediaPlayer here. The first is the autoPlay property. Setting autoPlay to true will let the media file play without the user's intervention. The second property is cycleCount, which tells the MediaPlayer how many times to play the current Media.

```
_player.setAutoPlay(true);
_player.setCycleCount(MediaPlayer.INDEFINITE);  \
```

Finally, set the MediaView to use the new MediaPlayer, and you are all set to play:

```
this.setMediaPlayer(_player);
```

The completed MyMediaView class should look as follows:

```
package Chapter14;

import javafx.scene.media.Media;
import javafx.scene.media.MediaPlayer;

/**
 *
 * @author J F DiMarzio
 */
public class MyMediaView extends MediaView {
    private MediaPlayer _player;
    private Media _media;
```

```
    public MyMediaView()
    {
        _media = new
Media("http://download.oracle.com/otndocs/products/javafx/oow2010-2.
flv");
        _player = new MediaPlayer(_media);
        _player.setAutoPlay(true);
        _player.setCycleCount(MediaPlayer.INDEFINITE);
        this.setMediaPlayer(_player);

    }
}
```

Now you can use MyMediaView to stream this video in your app. Let's add a MyMediaView to Chapter14.java, as follows:

```
package Chapter14;

import javafx.application.Application;
import javafx.scene.Group;
import javafx.scene.Scene;
import javafx.stage.Stage;

/**
 *
 * @author J F DiMarzio
 */
public class Chapter14 extends Application {

    /**
     * @param args the command line arguments
     */
    public static void main(String[] args) {
        launch(args);
    }

    @Override
    public void start(Stage primaryStage) {

        MyMediaView mp = new MyMediaView();

        Group root = new Group();
        root.getChildren().add(mp);
        primaryStage.setScene(new Scene(root, 540, 209));
        primaryStage.show();
    }
}
```

This code is pretty self-explanatory. You are creating a MyMediaView (the MediaPlayer you created earlier in the section) and placing it in your Scene.

Compile and run this example. You will see a sample video begin to play as soon as the application is loaded. The file plays automatically because you set the autoPlay property to true.

If you look a little more closely at the video playback, you may notice that it is very simplistic: There are no controls for playing and pausing the video. There are also no controls to indicate the progress of the video or to allow the user to skip through the video at will. In short, there are no controls whatsoever in the playback window.

To give your users control over the playback of a video, you will write the controls yourself. In the remainder of this section, you write some controls on your MediaPlayer and present them to the user.

TIP

Because you thought ahead and already created a custom MediaPlayer, the process for creating your controls will be much easier.

Let's create a quick button to control the playback of the video.

Creating a Play/Pause Button

In this section you create a play/pause button using the RoundButton custom button you created earlier in this book. If you do not have all the code for the RoundButton readily available, don't worry. The full RoundButton class and RoundButtonAPI should look like this (you can re-create it from here if needed):

```
package Chapter14;

/**
 *
 * @author J F DiMarzio
 */
public interface RoundButtonAPI {
    public static final int PLAY = 1;
    public static final int PAUSE = 2;

    public void setType(int type);
}
package Chapter14;

import javafx.scene.shape.Circle;
import javafx.scene.control.Button;

/**
 *
```

```
 * @author J F DiMarzio
 */
public final class RoundButton extends Button implements
RoundButtonAPI{

    @Override
    public void setType(int type) {
        Circle roundButtonClip = new Circle();
        roundButtonClip.setCenterX(18);
        roundButtonClip.setCenterY(12);
        roundButtonClip.setRadius(8);
        this.setClip(roundButtonClip);

        if(type == 1){
            this.setText(" >");
        }else{
            this.setText(" ||");
        }
    }

    public RoundButton(){
    }

    public RoundButton(int type)
    {
        this.setType(type);
    }

}
```

One cosmetic change has been made to this version of the RoundButton. The type indicator in this version of RoundButton has been changed from + or – to > or ||. This indicates whether the button is being used for playing the video or pausing the video, respectively.

TIP

If you need a refresher for how the RoundButton works, refer to Chapter 11.

Next, let's change one setting in your MyMediaView class. Change the autoPlay property from true to false, as shown next. This keeps the video from playing until you click the play button that will be added later.

```
package Chapter14;

import javafx.scene.media.Media;
import javafx.scene.media.MediaPlayer;
```

```
/**
 *
 * @author J F DiMarzio
 */
public class MyMediaView extends MediaView {
    private MediaPlayer _player;
    private Media _media = new
Media("http://download.oracle.com/otndocs/products/javafx/oow2010-2.
flv");

    public MyMediaView()
    {
        _player = new MediaPlayer(_media);
            _player.setCycleCount(MediaPlayer.INDEFINITE);
        this.setMediaPlayer(_player);

    }
}
```

Now that the button is ready, we need a way for it to hook into MyMediaView. The play() and pause() methods are contained within the MediaPlay; however, your MyMediaView extends MediaView, which is just a container. So, how do you control the playback? Easy. You are going to create a new interface that allows your MyMediaView to expose the MediaPlayer play() and pause() methods.

You created an interface in Chapter 11 for RoundButton. Create a new interface for this project named MyMediaViewAPI. The interface should have two methods, playMedia() and pauseMedia(), as shown here:

```
package Chapter14;

/**
 *
 * @author J F DiMarzio
 */
public interface MyMediaViewAPI {
    public void playMedia();
    public void pauseMedia();
}
```

Now, modify the MyMediaView class so that it implements the new MyMediaViewAPI. When you do so, NetBeans should add overrides for the two new methods.

```
package Chapter14;

import javafx.scene.media.Media;
import javafx.scene.media.MediaPlayer;
```

```
/**
 *
 * @author J F DiMarzio
 */
public class MyMediaView extends javafx.scene.media.MediaView implements
MyMediaViewAPI{
    private MediaPlayer _player;
    private Media _media = new
Media("http://download.oracle.com/otndocs/products/javafx/oow2010-2.flv");

    public MyMediaView()
    {
        _player = new MediaPlayer(_media);
        _player.setAutoPlay(false);
        _player.setCycleCount(javafx.scene.media.MediaPlayer.INDEFINITE);
        this.setMediaPlayer(_player);

    }

@Override
    public void playMedia() {

    }

    @Override
    public void pauseMedia() {

    }
}
```

Call the play() and pause() methods of the MediaPlayer from the playMedia() and pauseMedia() methods of MyMediaView, respectively:

```
@Override
    public void playMedia() {
        _player.play();
    }

    @Override
    public void pauseMedia() {
        _player.pause();
    }
```

Now you can call the playMedia() and pauseMedia() methods of MyMediaView directly from your app to control the playback of the file.

Add two RoundButtons to your Chapter14.java—one for play and one for pause:

```
package Chapter14;

import javafx.application.Application;
import javafx.scene.Group;
```

```
import javafx.scene.Scene;
import javafx.scene.layout.HBox;
import javafx.stage.Stage;

/**
 *
 * @author J F DiMarzio
 */
public class Chapter14 extends Application {

    /**
     * @param args the command line arguments
     */
    public static void main(String[] args) {
        launch(args);
    }

    @Override
    public void start(Stage primaryStage) {

        final MyMediaView mp = new MyMediaView();
        RoundButton play = new RoundButton(RoundButtonAPI.PLAY);
        RoundButton pause = new RoundButton(RoundButtonAPI.PAUSE);

        HBox hBox = new HBox();
        hBox.getChildren().add(play);
        hBox.getChildren().add(pause);

        Group root = new Group();
        root.getChildren().add(mp);
        root.getChildren().add(hBox);
        primaryStage.setScene(new Scene(root, 540, 209));
        primaryStage.show();
    }
}
```

The last step is to add two handlers (one for each RoundButton) that will call the respective method—playMedia() or pauseMedia()—of MyMediaView:

```
play.setOnAction(new EventHandler<ActionEvent>() {
@Override
    public void handle(ActionEvent event) {
        mp.playMedia();
    }
    });
pause.setOnAction(new EventHandler<ActionEvent>() {
@Override
    public void handle(ActionEvent event) {
        mp.pauseMedia();
    }
});
```

The full code of the Chapter14.java app should appear as follows:

```java
package Chapter14;

import javafx.application.Application;
import javafx.event.ActionEvent;
import javafx.event.EventHandler;
import javafx.scene.Group;
import javafx.scene.Scene;
import javafx.scene.layout.HBox;
import javafx.stage.Stage;

/**
 *
 * @author J F DiMarzio
 */
public class Chapter14 extends Application {

    /**
     * @param args the command line arguments
     */
    public static void main(String[] args) {
        launch(args);
    }

    @Override
    public void start(Stage primaryStage) {

        final MyMediaView mp = new MyMediaView();
        RoundButton play = new RoundButton(RoundButtonAPI.PLAY);
        RoundButton pause = new RoundButton(RoundButtonAPI.PAUSE);

        play.setOnAction(new EventHandler<ActionEvent>() {
            @Override
            public void handle(ActionEvent event) {
                mp.playMedia();
            }
        });
        pause.setOnAction(new EventHandler<ActionEvent>() {
            @Override
            public void handle(ActionEvent event) {
                mp.pauseMedia();
            }
        });

        HBox hBox = new HBox();
        hBox.getChildren().add(play);
        hBox.getChildren().add(pause);
```

```
        Group root = new Group();
     root.getChildren().add(mp);
  root.getChildren().add(hBox);
        primaryStage.setScene(new Scene(root, 540, 209));
        primaryStage.show();
     }
}
```

Compile and run this example. Your video will now load, but it will not play until you click the > button. Once the video plays, use the || button to pause.

Now that you have created a simple play/pause button, let's make a progress indicator that will also allow the user to advance and rewind the video.

Creating a Progress Indicator

To create a progress indicator, you need to know two key pieces of information. First, you need to know the total length of the video you are playing. Second, you need to know at what point in time of the playback you are currently. Luckily, JavaFX can tell you both of these things. However, it may take some massaging of the data to get it into a usable format.

You need to modify the MyMediaViewAPI to set up the interface to return these two pieces of data, plus add one more method that will allow you to indicate where you want the current time of the video to be set to.

Add the following to your MyMediaViewAPI interface:

```
package Chapter14;

/*
 * @author J F DiMarzio
 */
public interface MyMediaViewAPI {
    public void playMedia();
    public void pauseMedia();
    public void setCurrentTime(double time);
    public double getTotalRunTime();
    public double getCurrentTime();
}
```

When this is implemented in MyMediaView, you will be able to set the current time of the video, get the current time of the video, and get the total run time of the video. Save the interface and go back to the MyMediaView class. If you are using NetBeans, it should automatically detect that your interface has changed and create the overrides for you. They should be stubbed as follows:

```
package Chapter14;

import javafx.scene.media.Media;
import javafx.scene.media.MediaPlayer;
import javafx.util.Duration;

/**
 *
 * @author J F DiMarzio
 */
public class MyMediaView extends javafx.scene.media.MediaView implements
MyMediaViewAPI{
    private MediaPlayer _player;
    private Media _media = new
Media("http://download.oracle.com/otndocs/products/javafx/oow2010-2.flv");

    public MyMediaView()
    {
        _player = new MediaPlayer(_media);
        _player.setAutoPlay(false);
        _player.setCycleCount(javafx.scene.media.MediaPlayer.INDEFINITE);
        this.setMediaPlayer(_player);

    }

    @Override
    public void playMedia() {
        _player.play();
    }

    @Override
    public void pauseMedia() {
        _player.pause();
    }

@Override
    public void setCurrentTime(double time) {
    }

    @Override
    public double getTotalRunTime() {
    }

    @Override
    public double getCurrentTime() {
    }

}
```

Let's look at getCurrentTime() first. Within the MediaPlayer is a method, getCurrentTime(), that returns a Duration value. In the new getCurrentTime() method that you just created for MyMediaView, simply return the value of the MediaPlayer's getCurrentTime() converted to milliseconds:

```
@Override
public double getCurrentTime() {
    return _player.getCurrentTime().toMillis();
}
```

The toMillis() method of Duration translates the duration into milliseconds. Milliseconds are much easier to work with and are much more flexible than a Duration object.

Next, you can use the Media file itself to find out its total running time. In the getTotalRunningTime() method, return the value of getDuration() from the Media file, converted to milliseconds once again:

```
@Override
public double getTotalRunTime() {
    return _media.getDuration().toMillis();
}
```

Finally, finish out the modification to MyMediaView by adding some code to the setCurrentTime() method. The MediaPlayer has a method in it named seek(). This method lets you set the time in the video that you want the player to jump to. The seek() method accepts a Duration, so you will need to convert the double value you send into a Duration before you can pass it to seek().

```
@Override
    public void setCurrentTime(double time) {
        Duration setTime = new Duration(time);
        _player.seek(setTime);
    }
```

Save your modified MyMediaView and let's modify Chapter14.java to use this new functionality.

The control you will be using as your progress indicator is a Slider. The position of the Slider's toggle is controlled by a value property that uses doubles not Durations. Therefore, it would be much easier for you if you could convert the MediaPlayer's currentTime into a double; hence the extra work in the MyMediaView.

First, create a new Slider in your Chapter14.java:

```
final Slider progressBar = new Slider();
```

Now let's set the initial parameters of the Slider: the Max value (the highest value on the bar), the Min value (the lowest value on the bar), and the Value (the current position of the slider).

Given that the video doesn't start playing until the user clicks the play button, you can set these initial values in the event handler for this button.

```
play.setOnAction(new EventHandler<ActionEvent>() {
        @Override
        public void handle(ActionEvent event) {
            mp.playMedia();
progressBar.setMax(mp.getTotalRunTime());
            progressBar.setMin(0);
            progressBar.setValue(mp.getCurrentTime());
        }
    });
```

This is the complex part. You need to write a listener for the progressBar that will fire every time you move the slider. It will then write the current value of the progressBar to MyMediaView—using the setCurrentTime() method—to let the user manually advance and rewind the video.

Add a listener to the valueProperty of the progressBar. This will allow you to execute code when the value is changed by moving the slider.

```
progressBar.valueProperty().addListener(new InvalidationListener() {
        @Override
        public void invalidated(Observable arg0) {
if (progressBar.isValueChanging()) {
                mp.setCurrentTime((progressBar.getValue()));
            }
        }
});
```

Finally, you need to add a way for MyMediaView to update the slider's position on the progressBar. This can be accomplished using another property listener. This time you will listen for changes in the MediaPlayer's currentTime. When currentTime changes, you want to update the value of the progressBar, thus moving the slider forward as the video plays.

```
mp.getMediaPlayer().currentTimeProperty()
  .addListener(new InvalidationListener()
      {
        @Override
        public void invalidated(Observable arg0) {
            progressBar.setValue(mp.getCurrentTime().toMillis());
```

```
            }
        });
```

You now have the values needed to get and set the current playback time of the video. The full Chapter14.java file should now look like this:

```java
package Chapter14;

import javafx.application.Application;
import javafx.beans.InvalidationListener;
import javafx.event.ActionEvent;
import javafx.event.EventHandler;
import javafx.scene.Group;
import javafx.scene.Scene;
import javafx.scene.control.Slider;
import javafx.scene.layout.HBox;
import javafx.stage.Stage;

/**
 *
 * @author J F DiMarzio
 */
public class Chapter14 extends Application {

    /**
     * @param args the command line arguments
     */
    public static void main(String[] args) {
        launch(args);
    }

    @Override
    public void start(Stage primaryStage) {
        final Slider progressBar = new Slider();
        final MyMediaView mp = new MyMediaView();
        RoundButton play = new RoundButton(RoundButtonAPI.PLAY);
        RoundButton pause = new RoundButton(RoundButtonAPI.PAUSE);

        play.setOnAction(new EventHandler<ActionEvent>() {
            @Override
            public void handle(ActionEvent event) {
                mp.playMedia();
                progressBar.setMax(mp.getTotalRunTime());
                progressBar.setMin(0);
                progressBar.setValue(mp.getCurrentTime());
            }
        });
```

```
        pause.setOnAction(new EventHandler<ActionEvent>() {
            @Override
            public void handle(ActionEvent event) {
                mp.pauseMedia();
            }
        });

        progressBar.valueProperty().addListener(new
InvalidationListener() {
            @Override
            public void invalidated(javafx.beans.Observable arg0) {
                if (progressBar.isValueChanging()) {
                    mp.setCurrentTime((progressBar.getValue()));
                }
            }
        });

        mp.getMediaPlayer().currentTimeProperty().addListener(new
InvalidationListener()
        {
            @Override
            public void invalidated(javafx.beans.Observable arg0) {
                progressBar.setValue(mp.getCurrentTime());
            }
        });

        HBox hBox = new HBox();
        hBox.getChildren().add(play);
        hBox.getChildren().add(pause);
        hBox.getChildren().add(progressBar);

        Group root = new Group();
        root.getChildren().add(mp);
        root.getChildren().add(hBox);
        primaryStage.setScene(new Scene(root, 540, 209));
        primaryStage.show();
    }
}
```

Compile and run these classes. You now have a pause/play button and a progress indicator that allows the user to change the current playback position of the video.

In the final chapter of this book, you learn about using CSS to add even more originality to your UI.

Chapter 14 Self Test

1. What node is used to hold a MediaPlayer?

2. What package contains all the nodes needed to work with media files?

3. What property of the MediaPlayer tells the associated media object to play once it has loaded?

4. What media formats can the MediaPlayer play?

5. What method of the MediaPlayer will pause media playback?

6. True or false? MediaPlayer.mediaLength() will give you the total running time of a media file.

7. What type is MediaPlayer.currentTime?

8. What property of MediaPlayer can you bind to in controlling the playback volume?

Appendix A
Packaging and Deploying JavaFX

Much of this book was spent covering the basics of JavaFX development. You have learned how to navigate JavaFX APIs and create some very compelling applications. In this chapter, you are going to learn how to deploy the JavaFX applications you have created. There are three major methods for deploying JavaFX applications: using the JavaFX Packager tool, creating a self-contained app, and using the Web Start plug-in. Let's take a look at the JavaFX Packager tool in NetBeans.

JavaFX Packager Tool

Throughout this book you have created multiple JavaFX applications you can execute from within NetBeans. You have written some very useful applications in your short time with the APIs, but one issue remains: You need to be able to deploy the applications you write so that others can execute them.

The following steps teach you the first method for deploying applications: using NetBeans and the JavaFX Packager tool.

NOTE

In this example you will be using Chapter12.java. If you do not have Chapter12.java from the example in Chapter 12, any of the book's examples will work. In the event you have not retained any of the examples in the book, you may want to complete one before following these steps.

The first step in deploying JavaFX from NetBeans is to right-click your project in NetBeans and go to the project's Properties dialog box. From there, select the Run properties, as shown in Figure A-1.

In the Run properties, you just want to confirm that the Application Class setting is the correct class name of the .java file you want to execute. The class listed in the Application Class section is the file that will be compiled and deployed during this process. Once you have confirmed or set the correct class as the application class, you can close the project's Properties dialog box. Keep in mind that if you've never modified or tweaked the setting manually, there is no reason why this shouldn't already be set correctly.

The next step in deploying your JavaFX application is to build your project. The build process generates a .jar file that can be used to run the application outside the NetBeans IDE. To build your project, right-click your project once again and select Build Project, as shown in Figure A-2.

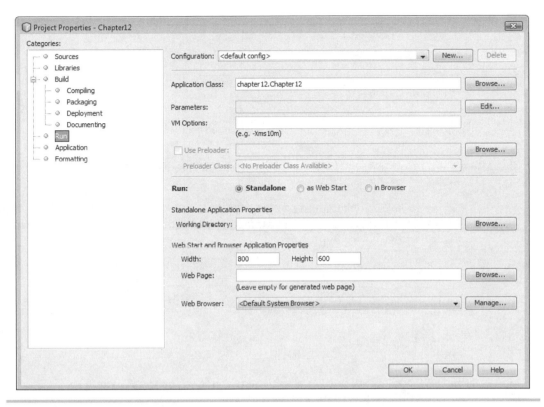

Figure A-1   Run properties

When the build process completes, you will have a .jar file containing the classes of your application. This .jar file, along with any other libraries you need, is placed in the dist folder of your NetBeans project. The contents of the dist folder are shown in Figure A-3.

Notice that one of the files created for you during the build process is an HTML file with the name of your project. This is a sample distribution file that contains all the information needed to distribute your app successfully. If you open the file, you will see that it contains the following code:

```
<html><head>
<SCRIPT src="./web-files/dtjava.js"></SCRIPT>
<script>
    function launchApplication(jnlpfile) {
        dtjava.launch(           {
            url : 'Chapter12.jnlp',
            jnlp_content : ''
        },
```

```
                    {
                        javafx : '2.0+'
                    },
                    {}
             );
             return false;
        }
    </script>

    <script>
        function javafxEmbed() {
            dtjava.embed(
                {
                    url : 'Chapter12.jnlp',
                    placeholder : 'javafx-app-placeholder',
                    width : 800,
                    height : 600,
                    jnlp_content : ''
                },
                {
                    javafx : '2.0+'
                },
                {}
            );
        }
    <!-- Embed FX application into web page once page is loaded -->
        dtjava.addOnloadCallback(javafxEmbed);
    </script>

    </head><body>
    <h2>Test page for <b>Chapter12</b></h2>
    <b>Webstart:</b><a href='Chapter12.jnlp' onclick="return
    launchApplication('Chapter12.jnlp');">click to launch this app as
    webstart</a><br><hr><br>

    <!-- Applet will be inserted here -->
    <div id='javafx-app-placeholder'></div>
    </body></html>
```

Within the script section of the HTML is a piece of JavaScript that allows the compiled project to run when this page is opened. Open the HTML file with your browser and you should see the fully functional application, as shown in Figure A-4.

In this short appendix you learned how to compile and build your .java files so that they can be executed outside of the NetBeans IDE. As you can see, the distribution process is very easy—which only adds to the usefulness and accessibility of JavaFX.

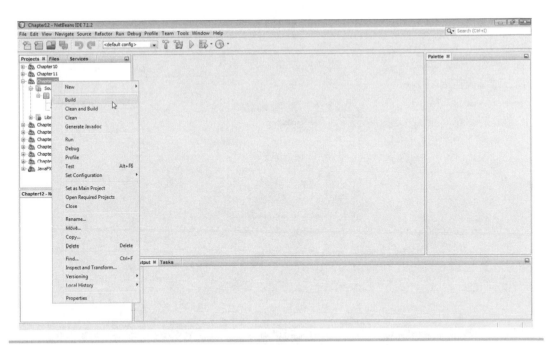

Figure A-2   Build Project

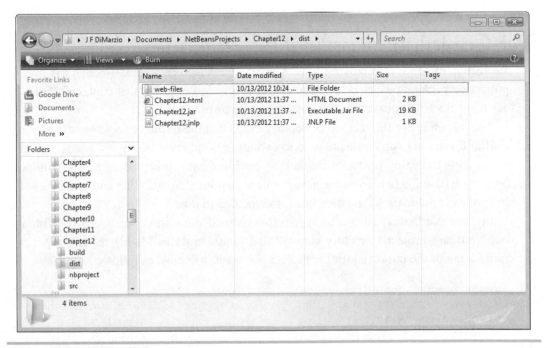

Figure A-3   The dist folder

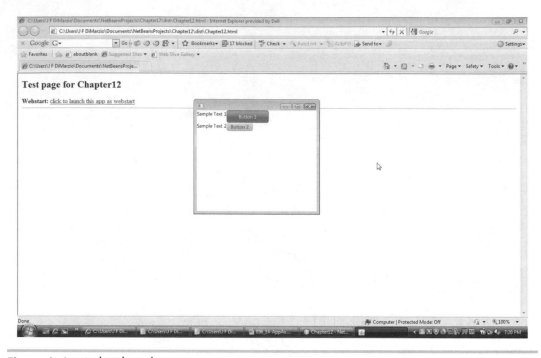

Figure A-4 A distributed app

Self-Contained Application Packages

The second method for deploying JavaFX applications is to create a self-contained application package, which is an executable file (.exe in Windows) that contains all the files needed to run your application on the target platform.

The advantage to this method of deployment is that the resulting package is in a familiar format to people who are used to executing Windows-based applications. If you are planning to deploy your application in an environment that is predominantly Windows application based, where users are going to be accustomed to installing and using these kinds of executable packages, then this is the method to use.

Luckily, NetBeans makes creating a self-contained application package easy. Within your NetBeans project's directory you will find a build.xml file. Modify the existing <target> tag of the build.xml for the project you want to deploy, as follows:

```
<target name="-post-jfx-deploy">
<fx:deploy width="${javafx.run.width}" height="${javafx.run.height}"
nativeBundles="all"
```

```
                    outdir="${basedir}/${dist.dir}"
outfile="${application.title}">
<fx:application name="${application.title}"
                        mainClass="${javafx.main.class}"/>
<fx:resources>
<fx:fileset dir="${basedir}/${dist.dir}"
                        includes="*.jar"/>
</fx:resources>
<fx:info title="${application.title}"
                vendor="${application.vendor}"/>
</fx:deploy>
</target>
```

These instructions will produce a self-contained application package in the form of an .exe file.

Web Start

JavaFX includes the option to deploy your applications as a Web Start, mainly to keep compatibility with older platforms. Deploying your application as a Web Start is very easy and can be accomplished by clicking one option.

Within NetBeans, right-click on the project and go to the project properties. Under the Run option, click the "Run: as Web Start" option. Now, when the application is deployed, the code for running as a Web Start will be added to the <application name>.html file in the dist folder.

Appendix B
The Swing of Things

Much of this book was spent covering the basics of JavaFX development. You have learned how to navigate JavaFX development and create some very compelling applications.

Admittedly, you have only scratched the surface of what is available to you in JavaFX, which is a very deep language with a lot to offer. No doubt, you have some questions about some of the things you have learned. This is the second of three appendixes that attempt to fill in some of the holes that may have been left in the lessons of this book. In this appendix we briefly cover the basics of JavaFX and Swing compatibility.

JavaFX Swing Compatibility

JavaFX 8 has provided you with a new node type that is used for JavaFX-to-Swing compatibility. The SwingNode node takes an instance of a Swing component and then writes the component to the screen using the setContent() method.

Because SwingNode inherits from node, it can be used anywhere node can be used. In the example that follows, a JLabel is placed in a JavaFX 8 app using a SwingNode. Start with an empty app:

```
public static void main(String[] args) {
        launch(args);
    }

    @Override
    public void start(Stage primaryStage) {
    }
```

Now instantiate a SwingNode:

```
public static void main(String[] args) {
        launch(args);
    }

    @Override
    public void start(Stage primaryStage) {
final SwingNode swingNode = new SwingNode();
    }
```

With the SwingNode instantiated, pass the setContent() method a new JLabel:

```
public static void main(String[] args) {
        launch(args);
    }

    @Override
    public void start(Stage primaryStage) {
final SwingNode swingNode = new SwingNode();
```

```
        swingNode.setContent(new JLabel("Swing Swing Swing"));
    }
```

Finish up the app as follows, and you will a JavaFX application with a Swing JLabel:

```
public static void main(String[] args) {
        launch(args);
    }

    @Override
    public void start(Stage primaryStage) {
final SwingNode swingNode = new SwingNode();
        swingNode.setContent(new JLabel("Swing Swing Swing"));
        StackPane pane = new StackPane();
        pane.getChildren().add(swingNode);

        primaryStage.setTitle("SwingNode Example");
        primaryStage.setScene(new Scene(pane, 400, 200));
        primaryStage.show();
    }
```

Adding Swing to your JavaFX applications is quite easy in JavaFX 8 and gives you a much greater level of flexibility.

One of the more useful features of the SwingNode is its ability to give you an easy upgrade path for existing applications. If you have already invested a great amount of time in some existing Swing apps, you can ease your upgrade cycle by incorporating those components into new JavaFX apps as a transition.

Putting JavaFX in Swing Apps

JavaFX and Swing interoperability is not a one-way street. In fact, you can include JavaFX content in your existing Swing apps. This is the perfect way to integrate new content in existing apps and extend their life and usability.

The JFXPanel, which inherits from JComponent, can be used to insert JavaFX content into your Swing application:

```
final JFXPanel javaFxPanel = new JFXPanel();
```

In much the same way that the key to a SwingNode is the setContent() method, the key to adding JavaFX content to a JFXPanel is the setScene() method:

```
Scene myScene = createScene();
javaFxPanel.setScene(myScene);
```

In the preceding snippet, myScene can be added to just like any JavaFX scene. This allows your JavaFX content to be integrated into your existing Swing apps.

Appendix C
Answers to Self Tests

Chapter 1

1. What is the name of the open-source development environment you will use throughout this book?
NetBeans.

2. True or false? You should download the version of NetBeans for All Developers.
False. You just need the version for Java SE bundle.

3. True or false? The Java JDK will be installed for you automatically if needed (if you have the JRE installed).
True.

4. Which NetBeans settings can you accept the default values for during installation?
The default NetBeans IDE path and the Java JDK installation path.

5. What is the difference between the JavaFX SDK and the Java JDK?
The Java JDK is used to develop and compile in Java. The JavaFX SDK is based on the Java JDK and is used for JavaFX development.

6. What is the purpose of the NetBeans start page?
The purpose of the NetBeans start page is to offer you tips and news about developing in NetBeans and JavaFX.

7. True or false? You must successfully register NetBeans before using it.
False.

8. At what website is NetBeans available?
www.netbeans.org.

9. Name two other applications that closely resemble the functionality of JavaFX.
Adobe Flash and Microsoft Silverlight.

10. True or false? JavaFX is developed in JavaFX Script.
False. JavaFX is now developed in Java. In older versions of JavaFX development was done in JavaFX Script.

Chapter 2

1. What is the name of the frame where all your projects are listed?
Projects.

2. What is the name of the wizard used to create a new JavaFX project?
The New JavaFX Project Wizard.

3. **What is another name for a namespace?**
   A package.

4. **Which panel of the NetBeans IDE lets you navigate through code samples?**
   The Palette.

5. **True or false? The Palette panel contains predefined pieces of reusable code.**
   True.

6. **What file extension is assigned to JavaFX code files?**
   .java.

7. **What type of word is "package" in the Java language?**
   A keyword, or reserved word.

8. **What markup language is FXML based on?**
   XML.

9. **What are the beginning and ending characters for comments?**
   /* and */.

10. **True or false? You cannot use a code-behind file when using FXML.**
    False, all of the elements in the .fxml file can call back to another code-based file.

Chapter 3

1. **What is the purpose of the MVC pattern?**
   MVC allows user interfaces to be designed and built independently of the logic that will be used to control it.

2. **What does MVC stand for?**
   Model View Controller.

3. **In JavaFX, what part of MVC does the FXML represent?**
   The View.

4. **What tool is used to edit FXML files?**
   JavaFX Scene Builder.

5. **What is binding in JavaFX?**
   Binding is a concept whereby you can link properties and values in such a way that the property is dynamically updated with the value changes.

6. **True or false? The syntax for binding is #{value}.**
   False, the syntax used in binding is ${value}.

7. **What is the $ operator known as in JavaFX?**
   The variable resolution operator.

8. **What is a method in Java?**
   A method in Java is a piece of code that can be called on by other pieces of code to perform a specific function.

9. **What is a property in JavaFX?**
   A property is a key:value pair that allows you to store and recall a piece of data.

10. **True or false? To bind to a property on a controller, you have to tell the FXML what file your property is in.**
    True, you will need to specify what file the property is in.

Chapter 4

1. **What layout organizes your nodes horizontally across a Scene?**
   HBox.

2. **True or false? The HBox is located in the javafx.scene package.**
   False. The HBox is located in the javafx.scene.layout package.

3. **What property holds the nodes for a layout to organize?**
   children.

4. **True or false? You must be sure to set the x- and y-coordinates of each node you place in a layout.**
   False. The layout takes care of the x- and y-coordinates for you.

5. **Can effects be applied to layouts?**
   Yes. Because layouts inherit from Node, they can use effects.

6. **What layout organizes nodes vertically down a Scene?**
   VBox.

7. **What is the name given to layouts that are combined to produce a new layout?**
   Nested layouts.

8. **True or false? For layouts to be nested, one must inherit from the other.**
   False. One layout simply needs to be added to the other's content.

9. **True or false? Only two layouts can be nested.**
   False. Multiple layouts can be nested.

10. **Name three layouts other than the VBox and HBox.**
    FlowPane, StackPane, and TilePane.

Chapter 5

1. **What four properties are needed to draw a line?**
   startX, startY, endX, and endY.

2. **How do you access the context menu?**
   CTRL-SPACE.

3. **What package is needed when working with colors?**
   javafx.scene.paint.

4. **What property controls the thickness of the line used to draw a shape?**
   strokeWidth.

5. **What package is needed to draw a polyline?**
   jaxafx.scene.shape.

6. **What type is assigned to the points property of a Polyline element?**
   An array.

7. **True or false? The height property of the Rectangle node is the number of pixels from the start point to the top of the rectangle.**
   False. The height attribute is the number of pixels from the start point *down*.

8. **What is the default value for the fill property of a Rectangle node?**
   Color.BLACK.

9. **True or false? RadiusX and radiusY comprise the point where the radius extends to.**
   False. RadiusX and radiusY are the radial lengths along the x- and y-axes, respectively.

10. **What property configures the radius of a circle?**
    radius.

Chapter 6

1. **How many predefined colors are available in the Color class?**
   148.

2. **What are the three methods available in the Color class for mixing colors?**
   Color.rgb, Color.hsb, and Color.web.

3. **True or false? RGB stands for refraction, gradient, and blur.**
   False. RGB stands for red, green, and blue.

4. **What is the acceptable value range for Hue?**
   0–360.

5. **In what package is the code for LinearGradients?**
   javafx.scene.paint.

6. **What is the default value for the proportional parameter?**
   True.

7. **What is the acceptable range of values for startX when proportional is set to true?**
   0–1.

8. **True or false? The stops parameter tells the gradient what point to stop on.**
   False. The stops parameter is an array of colors and the corresponding indications of where they are in the gradient.

9. **True or false? Gradients can be composed of more than two colors.**
   True.

10. **Which gradient is best for curvilinear shapes?**
    RadialGradients.

Chapter 7

1. **What node is used to display images?**
   ImageView.

2. **What class is used to write an image to the ImageView node?**
   Image().

3. **True or false? An Image class can accept images from the Web.**
   True.

4. **What protocol is used to locate an image in a local directory?**
   The file: protocol.

5. **True or false? To have an image load in the background, use the BackgroundImage loader.**
   False. Instead, set the backgroundLoading parameter of the constructor to true.

6. **What method allows you to move an image on the x-axis?**
   setTranslateX().

7. **What class contains the method setRotate(): Image or ImageView?**
   ImageView.

8. **What node is used to display images from an Image class?**
   ImageView.

9. **True or false? The setTranslateY() method moves an image a specified number of inches across the screen.**

False, it moves a number of pixels.

10. **What is the purpose of the setPreserveRatio() method?**

The setPreserveRatio() method ensures that the ratio of the image's size is preserved during scaling.

Chapter 8

1. **What package needs to be included to work with effects in JavaFX?**

javafx.scene.effect.

2. **What effect adjusts only the higher contrast areas of your node to make them glow?**

Bloom.

3. **True or false? All the parameters of ColorAdjust default to 0 if they are not specified.**

False. Contrast defaults to 1.

4. **What parameter needs to be specified to create a GaussianBlur effect?**

radius.

5. **What is the difference between Glow and Bloom?**

Glow is applied to the entire image, whereas Bloom only applies to the areas of higher contrast.

6. **True or false? You do not need to specify both a radius and a height/width for a DropShadow.**

True.

7. **Which effect takes all the opaque areas of your image and makes them transparent?**

InvertMask.

8. **What are the three different lights that can be used in the Lighting Effect?**

Light.Distant, Light.Point, and Light.Spot.

9. **What does the following code do?**

```
imageView.setRotate(45);
```

It rotates the image 45 degrees.

10. **How many parameters need to be set to create a PerspectiveTransform effect?**

Eight.

Chapter 9

1. Why is timing important to animation?
Timing is critical to producing smooth animation.

2. What controls the timer in JavaFX animation?
A Timeline.

3. True or false? A Timeline contains a child collection of KeyFrames.
True.

4. How do you start the Timeline?
Use .play() or playFromStart().

5. True or false? A keyframe is a point at which you want one or more keyvalues to be set to defined values.
True.

6. Which property of Animation sets the number of times a Timeline executes?
cycleCount.

7. What is the purpose of ArcTo?
ArcTo draws an arc from the last position of the point being used.

8. A path is created from a group of what?
PathElements.

9. What builder class is used to create an animation from a path?
PathTransitionBuilder().

10. Which PathTransition.OrientationType will change the orientation of the node as it moves along the path?
ORTHOGONAL_TO_TANGENT.

Chapter 10

1. True or false? The onMouse* properties are properties of the Node class.
True.

2. When is onMouseEntered fired?
When the mouse pointer enters the Node to which the event listener is attached.

3. True or false? The mouse-released **listener method will be called when the mouse is dragged.**
True. Mouse-released is only called when onMousePressed is followed by onMouseDragged.

4. True or false? Any class that inherits from Node can register listeners for mouse events.
True.

5. When events are used, what is the purpose of an anonymous inner class?
The purpose of an anonymous inner class is to immediately perform an action when the event is fired.

6. Which mouse event listener is called when the mouse pointer exits the node to which the event listener is attached?
onMouseExited.

7. What three events listener methods are called when the user interacts with the keyboard?
onKeyPressed, onKeyReleased, and onKeyTyped.

8. In what order are the key event listener methods called?
onKeyPressed, onKeyTyped, and then onKeyReleased.

9. What property will allow a node to accept focus?
focusTraversable.

10. True or false? The navigational buttons will fire the onKeyTyped event.
True.

Chapter 11

1. What process lets you take methods from one class and change their default behavior?
Overriding.

2. When you're creating a class, what keyword forces your class to inherit the methods and properties of another?
extends.

3. In the following example, what will a call to YourDog.displayBreed print?

```
public class MyDog extends Dog {
@Override
public void displayBreed(){
     System.out.println("Elkhound");
 }
}
public class YourDog extends Dog{
}
```
Elkhound.

4. **True or false? Ensuring that your files are all in the same package will make referencing them easier.**
   True.

5. **True or false? The process of inheriting from another class is known as subclassing.**
   True.

6. **What keyword do you use to implement an interface?**
   implements.

7. **True or false? You instantiate custom created nodes the same way you would instantiate a standard one?**
   True. All classes/nodes are instantiated the same way.

8. **What is the purpose of an HBox?**
   The purpose of an HBox is to automatically lay out nodes horizontally.

9. **What keyword annotation, beginning with @, can be used to change the default functionality of an inherited method?**
   @Override.

10. **True or false? Creating a API interface for your custom classes is a good coding procedure.**
    True. You should follow good coding practice whenever possible.

Chapter 12

1. **What node is used to hold or render a web page in a JavaFX app?**
   WebView.

2. **What packages contain the nodes needed to work with WebView and WebEngine?**
   javafx.scene.web.

3. **What method of the WebEngine is used to load a web page into a WebView?**
   .load().

4. **True or false? JavaScript-to-JavaFX communication is prohibited within JavaFX.**
   False.

5. **What method is used to execute a JavaScript against a page loaded in the WebView?**
   .executeScript().

Chapter 13

1. What is Cascading Style Sheets (CSS)?
CSS is a styling language that allows you to separate the styling elements of an object from the object itself.

2. What file extension is used for Cascading Style Sheets?
.css.

3. What wizard helps you create and add a CSS to your package?
The New File Wizard.

4. If you use the wizard to create your CSS, what class is added by default?
root.

5. True or false? To create a CSS class that applies to all nodes of a certain type, the name of the class should be the name of the node type in lowercase.
True.

6. What prefix is added to every Node property to call it from a CSS class?
-fx-.

7. What property of Scene will let you apply a style sheet to your script?
styleSheets.

8. True or false? You can only add one style sheet to a Scene.
False. You can add multiple style sheets to any particular Scene.

9. What Node property allows you to assign a specific CSS class to a node?
styleClass.

10. True or false? If you have a node with a node-applied CSS class and a styleClass property, the style in the styleClass will override that in the node-applied style.
True.

Chapter 14

1. What node is used to hold a MediaPlayer?
MediaView.

2. What package contains all the nodes needed to work with media files?
javafx.scene.media.

3. What property of the MediaPlayer tells the associated media object to play once it has loaded?
autoPlay.

4. **What media formats can the MediaPlayer play?**
MP3, MP4, and FLV.

5. **What method of the MediaPlayer will pause media playback?**
pause().

6. **True or false? MediaPlayer.mediaLength() will give you the total running time of a media file.**
False. MediaPlayer.media.duration.toMillis() will give you the running time in milliseconds.

7. **What type is MediaPlayer.currentTime?**
Duration.

8. **What property of MediaPlayer can you bind to in controlling the playback volume?**
volume.

Index

T

Reach More than 700,000 Oracle Customers with Oracle Publishing Group

Connect with the Audience that Matters Most to Your Business

Oracle Magazine
The Largest IT Publication in the World
Circulation: 550,000
Audience: IT Managers, DBAs, Programmers, and Developers

Profit
Business Insight for Enterprise-Class Business Leaders to Help Them Build a Better Business Using Oracle Technology
Circulation: 100,000
Audience: Top Executives and Line of Business Managers

Java Magazine
The Essential Source on Java Technology, the Java Programming Language, and Java-Based Applications
Circulation: 125,000 and Growing Steady
Audience: Corporate and Independent Java Developers, Programmers, and Architects

For more information or to sign up for a FREE subscription:
Scan the QR code to visit Oracle Publishing online.